Workb

of
Becky Kennedy's Book

Good Inside

A Guide to Becoming the Parent You Want to Be.

Created
By

Cosmic Publications

Note to Readers

This is an unofficial workbook outline & analysis of Dr. Becky Kennedy's book *"Good Inside"* designed to enrich your reading experience. Buy the original book on Amazon.

Cosmic Publications have not added or removed any information that would change or indicate a different view other than the views and opinions expressed by the author of the original work.

OUR FREE GIFT TO YOU

We understand that you didn't have to buy our summary, but because you did, we are very happy to give you something absolutely free.

Scan the QR Code to get free Access.

Contents

How to Use This Workbook

Our workbook is designed to accompany the original book by the original author. With that said, we strongly encourage you to purchase the original to get everything you can from our workbook.

Cosmic Publications has done its absolute best to bring you a comprehensive workbook with outlined chapters of the original for your convenience and study. Here, you will find chapter overviews, goal statements, key takeaways, check for understanding questions, reflection questions, action plans, plus a Self-Evaluation writing section for your own personal thoughts and growth.

CHAPTER OVERVIEW: The chapter overview is intended to be a "birds-eye view" of the chapter. Its purpose is to give you a starting point to focus on the overall theme of the chapter.

GOAL STATEMENT: The goals statement is your declaration as to what you will accomplish after you have completed reading the original chapter and finished our corresponding workbook chapter material. We recommend reading this statement out loud as well as internalizing it. Read this statement frequently so that you don't lose sight of the purpose of the chapter you are currently studying.

CHAPTER SUMMARY: This portion is where you will refresh your knowledge on each chapter you have read from the original and should be reviewed as often as needed. Here we have taken the main points and takeaways from each chapter and have summarized them for your convenience and mental retention.

CHECK FOR UNDERSTANDING: In this section we provide simple True / False questions that will test your basic knowledge of the various topics discussed in the chapter. Use this as a baseline for your own comprehension as it will help with answering the following sections which are reflective in nature. Answers are provided in the reference section of the workbook.

REFLECTION QUESTIONS: Unlike the "Check for Understanding" section of the workbook, the reflection questions are not solely about the information in the chapter but are designed to help you reflect on the information on a personal level. The type of questions asked will bring out a thought-provoking inquiry, such as "How do you relate to the information?" "What do you think you have to do to achieve the result you are seeking." "Is the information covered encouraging, causing you to be nervous or excited?" We have designed this portion to be about you. So, we recommend you take the time to answer each one honestly, then after some time has passed, come back and answer them again to see where you are. Making photocopies of the questions may be helpful so that you can come back later and see your progress.

ACTION STEP: It's not enough to just read and write about the lessons learned in the book but to act so that you can begin to improve your life. In the action plan, we recommend attempting the activity within 24 hours of reading the chapter or as soon as an opportunity arises.

We highly recommend spending at least one week trying to accomplish the action step. The action step is your opportunity to establish a new norm for yourself, so don't take it lightly. Be brave and begin to implement the information provided. The action step is where the rubber meets the road. You can do it.

SELF-EVALUATION: Accountability is essential when trying to make yourself better. In the self-evaluation section, write your experience with each chapter. How did it go? Did you have difficulties? Did you accomplish what you set out to do? Did you achieve the Goal Statement? Write your thoughts and feelings about what you were able to do with the lesson of the chapter. We hope that this section will be full of positive statements and helpful self-critique if need be.

FINALLY: It is our opinion that each chapter, along with its corresponding workbook material, be done on a per-week basis. If you can focus on one chapter per week and implement the action plan every day, you are more likely to maintain it beyond the workbook. You can change this to a few days if you prefer, but whatever you decide, stick to it. You got this!

Good Inside in a "Nutshell"

The book is a parenting guide for parents who want to improve as parents and want to make a positive impact on their children's lives. The book talks about how everyone, including you and your kids, is good inside. If that is the basic assumption you work with, it takes away all the judgments and blames from your action. What remains is empathy, love, and compassion.

The author talks about how the early years of one's life are formative years and how parenting can have a lot of impact on the kind of adults kids become. However, it's never too late and you can start the repair even now. While you might think of happiness as the ultimate goal, as parents, you should focus on raising kids who are resilient in the face of the challenges of life.

The book then goes on to talk about behavior and how it is not an indicator of your kid's identity. Their behavior is only a symptom of what's going on inside them. And to bring that out, you need to reduce shame and increase the connection. Once you do that, they will open up. In all of these efforts though, you should never forget to take care of yourself. Self-care will refill you for the challenging task of parenting that you must perform regularly.

The book also discusses the less-than-ideal behavior that your kid might often indulge in. The key to addressing that issue is not to directly target the behavior change. Instead, you must build connection capital with them, which you can later use to effect the behavior change. In all, you must learn to be empathetic towards your kids, make them feel loved at all times, and grow them into people who are confident and compassionate. The challenges in the parenting journey will be many and with this book, the author seeks to provide a useful tool to add to your parenting arsenal.

Chapter 1:
Good Inside

Chapter Overview

The chapter talks about how each one of us, including our kids, is inherently good inside. While due to various needs, our behaviors might be less than ideal in some instances, it doesn't define who we are. This chapter talks about how you can accept the idea that your child is a good human being having a hard time.

Read ahead to understand more about it.

Goal Statement

"I will learn to separate my child's identity from their behavior by accepting the good inside them."

Chapter Summary

The author has a basic assumption that we all, at our core, are compassionate, loving, and generous. This allows him to be curious about the bad behaviors and helps him develop frameworks and strategies that can effect change. This can be an effective parenting approach as you don't allow frustration and anger to dictate your decisions.

In a tough parenting moment, it is common to unconsciously operate from a point of view of the internal badness of one's kids. You might ask them, "What's wrong with you?", thinking that they are purposefully defying you. Then, you might even start blaming yourself for getting triggered by that. At that moment, your basic focus is to control your kids, instead of trusting them.

Still, the good inside perspective doesn't mean that anything goes. It just allows you to distinguish a person from a behavior. Your kids' behavior is not a measure of who they are, but what they need. This understanding can help you preserve your relationship while also leading to impactful change. You trust in them, believe that they are capable, and show them the way. You provide them with a safe space where they can fail, learn, and grow without judgment.

Humans are wired with a negativity bias. It's reflexive for you to default to a less generous view. Even your childhood experiences influence how you perceive and respond to kids' behavior. In absence of an intentional effort, history repeats itself.

At various stages in life, we all behave in ways that are less than ideal. The early years however are especially important as they dictate how you respond to difficult situations. How you talk to yourself is also affected by how your parents talk to you in your early years. So, your parents' behavior decides the nature of your self-talk and your behavior with your kids as well.

In our early years, our primary goal is to get love. And our body keeps learning the conditions under which we receive love. Then, we began to adopt what's appreciated as good, and start rejecting what's rejected by our near ones.

Conclusively, no part of you or your child is bad. Under every bad behavior, there's a good child showing symptoms of pain, fear, and insecurity. It doesn't need judgment and punishment, but rather empathy and connection. Kids act how you paint them to be. So, if you keep telling them that they are selfish, they are going to behave that way. With the knowledge of this book, you can break a flawed intergenerational pattern. So, if you tell them good things about them, they behave that way and grow up to be more empathetic towards themselves. And remember to never aim for a perfect outcome with your kids. Instead, aim for growth.

Check for Understanding

1. Your kid's behavior reflects who they are.

   TRUE   **FALSE**

2. Humans have wired with a positive bias.

   TRUE   **FALSE**

3. Your child's bad behavior can be effectively addressed by building a connection with them.

   TRUE   **FALSE**

4. In a tough parenting moment, it's hard to view your kid as inherently good.

   TRUE   **FALSE**

5. When you believe in the internal goodness of your kid, you let them behave in whatever way they want.

   TRUE   **FALSE**

Reflection Questions

1. What's your reaction like when your kid is not behaving as you want them to?

_____

_____

_____

_____

_____

_____

_____

2. Do you believe that your kids are inherently good and have some hard moments when they struggle to behave?

_____

_____

_____

_____

_____

_____

_____

3. *Your kid's behavior is a measure of what they* need – Explain what you understand by this statement.

_____

_____

_____

_____

_____

_____

_____

4. How would you evaluate your relationship with your kid?

_____

_____

_____

_____

_____

_____

_____

Action Plan

1. Complete the "Rewiring the Circuit" exercise from the original book.

2. Whenever in a tough parenting situation, ask yourself "What is my most generous interpretation of what just happened?" This will help you understand what's going on inside your kid, even modeling a self-reflecting approach for them.

Self-Evaluation

What new did you learn in this chapter? Did the action plan help you better handle the tough parenting moments?

_____

_____

_____

_____

_____

_____

_____

_____

_____

_____

_____

_____

_____

_____

_____

_____

_____

_____

_____

_____

_____

_____

_____

Chapter 2:
Two things are true

Chapter Overview

The chapter talks about how there can be more than two truths. Like you could love your child and yet set firm boundaries for them. Once you embrace this fact, you can better manage your guilt while parenting. Also, you can better accept that your kids are not their behavior.

Read ahead to understand how two things are true thinking can help you.

Goal Statement

"I will learn to become a better parent by embracing the two things are true mode."

Chapter Summary

While parenting, you can both be fun and firm, silly and sturdy at once. You can parent with a firm set of expectations and still be playful. You can create and enforce boundaries while still caring for your kids' feelings. For this, you must accept the idea of multiplicity, i.e., the ability to accept that multiple things can be true at one. This ability allows two people with conflicting opinions to get along and have a healthy relationship. Understanding, and not convincing, is the key.

The goal of understanding is connection. When you are trying to understand, you accept that there isn't one correct interpretation of the situation. This is how you connect to your kids. On the other hand, convincing involves proving that there is a singular reality. In this approach, the other person feels unseen and unheard. It makes connection impossible. Contrarily, it makes the other person defensive as you turn judgemental. But understanding involves being curious and accepting of the other person's experience. This is a vital factor in building better relationships. It is true even for business leaders who listen to and validate their employees very often.

In "two things are true" mode, you notice the multiple feelings, thoughts, urges, and sensations inside you and still know that they are not you. Like, you can love your kids and still crave alone time. You can yell at your kids and still love them. You can make decisions that you know are good for your kids and still care about their feelings. There would always be multiple realities that can be best handled through acknowledgment. This mode can guide you into becoming better parents and sturdier adults.

Remember, at the core we all want someone to acknowledge our experience. Like, when your kid is defying you and you both are arguing about something, you both are essentially searching to feel seen. You want to be acknowledged for your needs while your kids want to be seen for theirs. Behave in a way that makes them feel seen and let them see you as a teammate, rather than an adversary. However, it doesn't mean backing down when the situation demands setting firm boundaries. But even in your unilateral decisions, remember to acknowledge your child's experience by naming it and allowing them to feel their feelings.

Parenting is a hard job, and you'll often want to fall into the "I am a bad parent, and I am messing up my kid" mentality. But that's a "one thing is true" approach. The "two things are true" approach would be "I am a good parent who's having a hard time." This allows you the room to make mistakes while you work hard at improving.

Check for Understanding

1. If you love your kid, you cannot set firm boundaries.

   TRUE   **FALSE**

2. If you want to be firm, you cannot be silly.

   TRUE   **FALSE**

3. Convincing your kids means you believe in the idea of a singular reality.

   TRUE   **FALSE**

4. Understanding is essential for building a connection with your kids.

   TRUE   **FALSE**

5. Understanding your kid's side means you are taking the "two things are true" approach.

   TRUE   **FALSE**

Reflection Questions

1. Do you set boundaries for your kid? How does it feel to you and to your kid?

   _____

   _____

   _____

   _____

   _____

_____

_____

2. Do you ever fall into the parenting guilt and self-blame trap? How do you manage it?

_____

_____

_____

_____

_____

_____

3. How often do you try to convince your kid that your point of view is correct and theirs's not?

_____

_____

_____

_____

_____

_____

_____

4. As a parent, how often do you try to understand your kid's point of view?

_____

_____

_____

_____

_____

_____

5. Do you know someone who validates others' points of view quite often in conversations? Why do you think they do so?

_____

_____

_____

_____

_____

_____

_____

Action Plan

1. In all your life relationships, make a conscious effort to stay in the "two things are true" mode for as long as possible.
2. When you fall into the self-blame trap, tell yourself "I am a good parent who's having a hard time."

3. Make it a conscious effort to make your kid feel and seen in a difficult situation.

Self-Evaluation

What new did you learn in this chapter? Did the action plan help you manage your guilt and become a better parent?

_____

_____

_____

_____

_____

_____

_____

_____

_____

_____

_____

_____

_____

_____

_____

_____

_____

_____

Chapter 3:
Know Your Job

Chapter Overview

The chapter talks about how individual jobs are predefined in a family system. Like it's a kid's job to be curious, explore, make mistakes, learn and grow. And it's a parent's job to provide a safe environment for the kid to be able to do so.

Read ahead to understand more about your job as a parent.

Goal Statement

"I will become a better parent by providing a safe & supportive environment for my kid to grow."

Chapter Summary

In any system, it's critical that roles and responsibilities are defined clearly to ensure that everything runs smoothly. Family is a system too and everyone has a job. It's a parent's job to establish safety through boundaries, validation, and empathy. Children have the job of exploring and learning through experiencing and expressing their emotions. However, some roles are prioritized over others. Like safety comes before happiness or your child's being pleased with you. If you give in to their emotional outburst, they receive an implicit message that no one can help them once they are out of control. But that's what they are looking for, some help from an adult to grow their emotion regulation skills.

The primary way to ensure safety is to set proper boundaries that protect your child and contain their behavior. For example, you don't let your toddlers walk too far from you on a sidewalk. That's a boundary. Children need such protection emotionally too. It is so because while they can fully experience all the emotions, they still don't have the capability to regulate them. That's why, in their initial developmental years, they are not able to make good decisions. Your goal is to help them, and while doing so teach them through experiences the way to manage their feelings. You shouldn't shut down their feelings ever. Remember that boundaries are not what you tell your kids not to do; they are what you tell your kids you will do. It embodies your authority and doesn't require any action from your child. For example, instead of telling your child to stop hitting their sibling, you could step in and say, "I will not let you do it". It might involve you gently holding their wrist to prevent any more hitting. Such a boundary is a form of love expressing that you know that the kid is good inside and is just having a hard, out-of-control time.

Additionally, as a parent, you have two other duties – validation & empathy. Validation means to acknowledge someone else's emotional experience as real and true. Invalidation means to dismiss someone's emotional experience. Validation will sound like, "You're upset, that's real, I see that." While invalidation would sound like, "There's nothing to be upset about. Stop being so sensitive." This doesn't help. Everyone needs to be seen for who they are and at any given moment, who we are is deeply related to our feelings at that moment.

Empathy is one's ability to understand and relate to the feelings of the other person. When you are empathetic towards your child, you approach their emotional experiences with curiosity and not judgment. It allows them to feel felt and thus they develop their capability to regulate their emotions. It makes it less likely for their feelings to manifest in their behavior.

Boundaries let your kids see that even the most difficult emotions can eventually be managed. Validation & empathy grounds them in their goodness. It allows them to experience their difficult emotions without being controlled by them. As kids, it is their job to struggle and learn, and when they are struggling and being difficult, know that they are doing their job.

Check for Understanding

1. Roles & responsibilities are clearly defined in a family system.

   TRUE   **FALSE**

2. As a parent, you must validate your kid's feelings.

   TRUE   **FALSE**

3. Empathy helps you approach others' emotions with curiosity rather than judgment.

   TRUE   **FALSE**

4. A boundary is what you tell your kid you will do if they violate a condition.

   TRUE   **FALSE**

Reflection Questions

1. What do you think your role is in your family? Elaborate.

_____

_____

_____

_____

_____

_____

_____

2. Do you find it easy to empathize with your kids? Cite real-life examples.

_____

_____

_____

_____

_____

_____

_____

3. What is your response like when your kid is having a hard feeling? Do you consciously validate their feelings? Explain in detail.

_____

_____

_____

_____

_____

_____

_____

4. Do you think you provide a safe learning environment for your kid? According to you, what constitutes a safe learning environment?

_____

_____

_____

_____

_____

_____

_____

Action Plan

1. Make it a point to set firm boundaries with your kids at home.

2. Validate your kids' emotions whenever they express them through any means. Empathize with them. But remember to check on your boundaries.

3. In a tough parenting situation, know that your child is just doing their job of being curious. Consciously reminding yourself will make you much less reactive.

Self-Evaluation

What new did you learn about your role in this chapter? Did the action plan help you better connect with your kid?

_____

_____

_____

_____

_____

_____

_____

_____

_____

_____

_____

_____

_____

_____

_____

_____

_____

_____

_____

_____

_____

_____

_____

_____

Chapter 4:
The Early Years Matter

Chapter Overview

The chapter talks about how the early years are the formative years for kids. Their early experiences are going to affect the kind of adults they grow up to become. The part that gets more acceptance in a kid gets amplified while the rejected ones get suppressed.

Read ahead to understand more about your kid's emotional development.

Goal Statement

"I will try to ensure the emotional development of my kids by giving them healthy experiences during their early years."

Chapter Summary

Even if the kids cannot remember, the early years of parenting matter as kids remember these years with their bodies if not with their memory. The early parents-kid interaction leaves a blueprint they use to interact with the world later on. It affects what part of themselves they feel ashamed of, what they hide from the world, and what feels loveable. A kid who's told not to be sensitive will think of feelings as wrong and would push people away.

But don't worry. The human brain can rewire and repair. So, you can still help your kid grow to be an emotionally healthy individual. To better understand why the early years matter so much, you must understand attachment theory and internal family systems.

Attachment theory says that children are wired to attach to individuals who provide the comfort and security they need to survive. This is a primary evolutionary mechanism. The early age experiences affect the internal working model of a child, i.e., their thoughts, memories, beliefs, expectations, emotions, and behaviors. This affects their relationships with themselves and others. In their early interactions, they try to answer questions like *Am I loveable? Do people like me to be around?* etc. So, while you might be saying no to a later bedtime, they take in whether it's safe, in any given relationship, to have the desires and feelings that lead to difficult moments. Such early childhood wirings impact how they think about themselves and others long after childhood. They adjust their behavior with the goal of establishing a secure attachment. Children often learn to shut down their feelings and experiences if pushed away or punished for their feelings.

If responded to with love and acceptance, even while having firm boundaries, your child will learn to regulate emotions and manage disappointments. In the long run, they will build self-trust, acceptance, and openness with others, avoiding shame and defensiveness. It is a thumb rule that the more a child feels safer and more with this parent, the safer and more secure he will be in his adult relationships. This will make him open to being vulnerable in his relationships.

A secure relationship with parents includes responsiveness, warmth, predictability, and repair when things feel bad. A child can get more curious, explorative, and independent if he can depend on his parent as a safe base.

Additionally, a lot of your behavior depends on your Internal family systems (IFS). It considers different parts of a person. Like you have a confident side, an anxious side, an angry side, a gentle side, etc. You are the sum of all of these parts. If you become reactive when one of these parts takes over, you lose your complete identity and become a singular feeling. The language of parts gives people freedom, compassion, relief, and the ability to regulate their experiences.

When combined, attachment theory and IFS give us a better understanding of our child's emotional development. Attachment theory says that the child seeks to increase attachment to ensure survival while IFS answers the questions like *"Which parts of me get more acceptance and can build better connections?"* Kids learn this through their experiences with their parents.

Check for Understanding

1. In healthy relationships, nothing ever goes bad.

    TRUE   **FALSE**

2. Repair is the foundation of healthy relationships.

    TRUE   **FALSE**

3. Attachment for children is a survivalist trait.

    TRUE   **FALSE**

4. It's never too late to improve your relationship with your kid.

    TRUE   **FALSE**

5. The human brain can be rewired at any stage to change how your life unfolds.

    TRUE   **FALSE**

Reflection Questions

1. What did you understand by the attachment theory? Try relating it to your real-life experiences.

    _____

    _____

    _____

    _____

    _____

    _____

    _____

2. What do you understand by the IFS theory? What do you know about your IFS?

    _____

    _____

    _____

    _____

    _____

    _____

    _____

3. What was your childhood like in terms of acceptance & boundaries? Explain in detail.

_____

_____

_____

_____

_____

_____

_____

4. Do you agree that the early years of life can have an immense effect on the development of a person? Why or why not?

_____

_____

_____

_____

_____

_____

_____

Action Plan

1. Make it a conscious choice to not compromise with the firm boundaries that you have set for your kid. Remember that you can show that you care for your kid's feelings and yet keep the boundaries intact.

2. Understand your IFS and tweak it to meet your kid's needs in whatever ways necessary.

Self-Evaluation

What did you learn about the importance of early years of life in your child's emotional development? Did the action plan help you give healthier experiences to your kid?

_____

_____

_____

_____

_____

_____

_____

_____

_____

_____

_____

_____

_____

_____

_____

_____

_____

_____

Chapter 5:
It's Not too Late

Chapter Overview

This chapter talks about how it is never too late to repair and reconnect with your children. The brain has an innate capacity to rewire. It is the same for the adult brain too. So, you can rewire yourself to become a better adult and parent.

Read ahead to understand the rewiring capacity of your brain.

Goal Statement

"I will learn to rewire with my kids by connecting with them better."

Chapter Summary

It's never too late to repair and reconnect with your kids. It's never too late to rewire yourself as an adult. You just have to repair your strategies with yourself first and then with your kids. Also, you must learn to manage the guilt of your past behaviors. Parenting is a tough task as it requires a huge among of self-reflection, learning, and evolving. With kids, we get confronted with so many truths that we must address to progress in our parenting job.

The brain is an amazing organ. It wires early in our childhood but has the amazing capacity to rewire too. If old ways do not serve you now, you can change them. An individual wired for insecure attachment can rewire for secure attachment. Even one's secure relationship with their therapist can benefit them in immense ways.

A child's brain gets wired according to his relationship with his parents. Not only that, but it changes in response to the environment as well. A neglectful environment leads it to shrink while an enriching environment makes it grow. A recent study revealed that appropriately targeted parenting programs have equal effectiveness for two- to eleven-year-old kids. So, it is never too early or too late for you to parent your kids right.

And it is not only your child that needs to change. It's you too. When a parent changes, so do the child as the parent's level of emotional maturity can dictate the struggles their child faces. So, it's your responsibility to evolve as well. But while doing so, remember that there is nothing such as a perfect parent. You can act out at times but your reconnection with your kid after the conflict is what defines your parenting.

If you don't reconnect with them, they either self-doubt or self-blame. In self-doubt, they began to deny and invalidate their own experience believing that they are overreacting. This wires them to stop trusting their feelings and use others' treatment of them to define their identity.

In self-blame, they start blaming themselves to feel in control. Once they do that, they know that if they change, the conflict won't be there anymore. This makes them feel that the environment they are in is already safe.

To avoid these two coping scenarios, parents should reconnect with their children. You won't always get everything right. But the worthiest goal here is to get good at repairing your bonds. This repair can happen any time after a blow-up but that shouldn't be your excuse to delay the work.

Check for Understanding

1. You must become a perfect parent to ace parenting.

   TRUE   **FALSE**

2. Self-doubt leads kids to invalidate their feelings.

   TRUE   **FALSE**

3. A parent's level of emotional maturity dictates the struggles that a kid face.

   TRUE   **FALSE**

4. Your brain can rewire even when you are an adult.

   TRUE   **FALSE**

Reflection Questions

1. After a conflict situation between you and your kid, who initiates the repair? How long after the conflict does the repair start? Elaborate.

   _____

   _____

   _____

   _____

   _____

   _____

   _____

2. How would you rate your growth environment as a child? Elaborate.

_____

_____

_____

_____

_____

_____

_____

3. What are the traits of an ideal parent according to you? How many of these do you have?

_____

_____

_____

_____

_____

_____

_____

4. What is your definition of a healthy relationship? Does it have room for a conflict?

_____

_____

_____

_____

_____

_____

_____

Action Plan

1. Remind yourself –

   • "I am working on myself and working to take care of my family."

   • "I am trying to rewire what doesn't help me or my kids."

2. The key element to good parenting is a connection after disconnection. Learn to say sorry to your kids when you are wrong. After a conflict, go to them un-defensively and share your reflections. Express your desire to have done things differently.

3. Constantly keep reminding yourself, "Good parents don't get it right all the time. Good parents repair."

Self-Evaluation

What new did you learn in this chapter? How did the action plan help you?

_____

_____

_____

_____

_____

_____

_____

_____

Are you enjoying the book so far?

If so, please help us reach more readers by taking 30 seconds to write just a few words on Amazon by using the QR code below

Or, you can choose to leave one later...

Scan me

Chapter 6:
Resilience > Happiness

Chapter Overview

The chapter talks about how parents try for their kids to be happy all the time. It's a good but not an ideal goal to have. If you want the best for your kids, you should instead aim at building resilience in them. At some point in life, there will be a time in your kid's life when things would be hard and it would be resilience that would help them get through such situations and achieve happiness.

Read ahead to understand how resilience can help your kid.

Goal Statement

"I will learn to ensure happiness for my kid by building their resilience."

Chapter Summary

You as a parent want your kids to be happy. But it is not possible if they cannot manage their emotions and cope with stress. Not only that, but people also even get stressed about stress. They take difficult emotions as negative and something that must be avoided at all costs. When they cannot do that, they feel stressed. That's why you must help your kid to build resilience.

Resilience lets us feel a range of emotions and still be ourselves. It helps us bounce back from every situation. It is a sound ground for happiness to take root in. Resilience doesn't mean you become immune to stress or struggle. It's no guarantee of success but it can guide your behavior when there's no confirmation of pending success. Rather, it defines how you relate to and experience difficult moments. Fortunately, it's a skill that can be learned.

You can develop resilience in your kids by – empathizing, listening, accepting them for who they are, being a safe and consistent presence, identifying their strengths, allowing them to make mistakes, helping them become responsible, and inculcating problem-solving skills in them.

As a parent, if you focus more on your child's happiness, you set them up for an adulthood of anxiety. In that approach, you start solving your kids' problems instead of teaching them how to address issues themselves. This is a short-sighted approach. Adults whose childhoods only focused on happiness never get prepared for the tough moments of life.

Check for Understanding

1. Your kids can stay happy even with zero emotional management.

   TRUE   **FALSE**

2. You should solve all your kids' problems as that is faster.

   TRUE   **FALSE**

3. You should allow your kids to make mistakes.

   TRUE   **FALSE**

4. Adults whose childhoods only focused on happiness never get to learn about coping with stress.

   TRUE   **FALSE**

Reflection Questions

1. Who is the most resilient person that you know? Cite some real-life examples of their resilience.

_____

_____

_____

_____

_____

_____

_____

2. Do you consider yourself a resilient person? Why or why not?

_____

_____

_____

_____

_____

_____

3. What is the most essential factor that determines happiness according to you? Which of these things do you try to ensure for your kids?

_____

_____

_____

_____

_____

_____

_____

4. Do you solve all your kid's problems or just guide them, letting them put in the work, make mistakes, and grow? What are your thoughts about it now?

_____

_____

_____

_____

_____

_____

_____

Action Plan

1. Whenever engaging with your kid on an issue, ask yourself, "Am I teaching him to avoid the problem or to work through the distress?" The latter one is desirable.

2. Make a conscious effort to be with your child when they are in distress.

3. Connect with your kid and be present in his experiences.

4. Teach your kid that discomfort is not something that is to be avoided but something that ensures your growth.

5. In difficult situations, encourage communication instead of teaching your kid to look the other way.

Self-Evaluation

What did you learn about resilience and happiness in this chapter? How did the action plan help you?

_____

_____

_____

_____

_____

_____

_____

_____

_____

_____

_____

_____

_____

_____

_____

_____

_____

_____

_____

_____

_____

_____

_____

_____

Chapter 7:
Behavior is a window

Chapter Overview

The chapter talks about how a person is not their behavior at any moment. However, behavior is an apt window into the feelings, thoughts, urges, needs, etc. of a person. Hence, if you are moving forward only with a behavior modification approach, the associated change isn't going to be long-lasting. Instead, building a connection with your kid and using that to effect change will generate permanent results.

Read ahead to understand how behavior is a window into your child's feelings.

Goal Statement

"I will learn to effect behavior change in my kids by building a meaningful connection."

Chapter Summary

Behavior is a symptom of what is going on inside someone. One's behavior is a window into the feelings, thoughts, urges, sensations, perceptions, unmet needs, and emotional pain of a person behaving that way. On the surface, you see the behavior, but inside is a person. As behavior is a symptom, trying to change it doesn't address the core issue.

For a long time, parents have only used the behavior-first approach. But that hasn't worked, as to behave better, children first need to feel better. Behavior modification interventions are temporary, and they don't help your children build any skills.

Such tactics might appear to succeed with a people-pleasing child, but that kid will suffer later as they will grow reluctance to say no, an inability to assert their need, and will keep prioritizing others wellness over their own needs. With non-people pleasers, these methods would worsen the challenging behavior.

These behavior-changing methods don't let you develop a meaningful relationship with your kid as you show indifference to their distress and personhood. Thus, when they grow up, you don't have leverage that you can use to affect any change in them.

Still, the parents use the behavior-first methods as they are tangible, clear, and easy to understand. Getting to the root of your kid's problem is hard work that you might not have the energy for. But the hard option is the right choice for you to make. So, when your child acts out, instead of punishing them for their behavior, you should focus on understanding them. You might think that it is akin to rewarding a misbehaving kid with positive attention. This will encourage them to behave in this way even more. But that's not so. It simply means that instead of reducing connection after a bad behavior incident, you should respond by increasing connection outside such behaviors.

Check for Understanding

1. You should encourage your child's bad behavior.

   TRUE   **FALSE**

2. Behavior modification tactics work best with people-pleasing children.

   TRUE   **FALSE**

3. Behavior-first approach might hinder your relationship with your kids.

   TRUE   **FALSE**

4. Behavior-first tactics are less tangible and thus harder to understand.

   TRUE   **FALSE**

Reflection Questions

1. What methods do you use to effect behavior change in your children?

   _____

   _____

   _____

   _____

   _____

   _____

   _____

2. Do you know someone who uses their relationship with their children to effect behavior change in them?

   _____

   _____

_____

_____

_____

_____

_____

3. Cite any behavior-changing tactics that you have seen parents employ but that don't work. Why do you think the failure happens?

_____

_____

_____

_____

_____

_____

_____

4. What do you seek to ultimately achieve by changing your kid's behavior? Answer with as much introspection as possible.

_____

_____

_____

_____

_____

_____

Action Plan

1. Be conscious about building a meaningful relationship with your kids.
2. While interacting with your kids, understand that behavior change is not the final goal. Neither it is the core issue. Rather, it is a symptom.
3. When your kid misbehaves, try understanding the real issue behind such behavior. This doesn't mean encouraging bad behavior.

Self-Evaluation

What did you learn about effecting behavior change in your kids? How did the action plan help?

_____

_____

_____

_____

_____

_____

_____

_____

_____

_____

_____

_____

_____

Chapter 8:
Reduce Shame, Increase Connection

Chapter Overview

The chapter talks about how shame leads children to behave in a dysregulated manner. It creates a gap between the kids and the parents that eventually harms the relationship. For that reason, parents should try to be more understanding of their children's behavior. This will build a better connection and lead to improved behavior in the future.

Read ahead to understand the dynamics of shame and connection.

Goal Statement

"I will learn to reduce shame for my child by building the connection."

Chapter Summary

A child struggling with the painful reality of being awful often chooses to shut down. This feeling of being awful and ashamed manifests in dysregulated behavior to avoid dealing with guilt or a bad feeling. Shame motivates people to hide, to distance themselves from others. For children, it elicits the threat of abandonment, which is an ultimate danger to their survival. Shame freezes a child as a protection mechanism and it emerges in their inability to apologize, in their reluctance to accept help, or an unwillingness to tell the truth. In such a situation, it is easier to misinterpret their behavior.

Hence, you should try to be less judgmental and more understanding as a parent. Instead, if you work to reduce the shame in a moment, you can equip your child with the ability to deal with such situations in the future. It will tell them that they are good inside and have worth. If the shame goes unchecked, they will suffer the long-term effects. They will struggle with opening up to their partners in their relationships, among other things.

However, if you build a good connection with them as a parent, that is going to help them. The connection doesn't mean approval of their behavior. It only means you connect to the person beneath that behavior and you trust that person to behave better once the core issue is addressed.

Check for Understanding

1. Children who feel ashamed of something tend to shut down.

   TRUE   FALSE

2. Understanding instead of judging can help you reduce shame for your child.

   TRUE   FALSE

3. Children might deny help when they feel ashamed.

   TRUE   FALSE

4. Your kids won't share their thoughts & feelings with you if you are too judgmental of them.

   TRUE   FALSE

Reflection Questions

1. Are you judgmental or understanding with your kid? Be honest. Cite real-life examples to justify.

_____

_____

_____

_____

_____

_____

2. What parts of you seek recognition, compassion, and permission to exist?

_____

_____

_____

_____

_____

_____

3. Who's the most judgmental person you know? How likely are you to communicate your truth, thoughts, and feelings to them?

_____

_____

_____

_____

_____

_____

_____

4. Is there any part of you that you are ashamed of? How would you react if that side is about to be revealed to the world?

_____

_____

_____

_____

_____

_____

_____

Action Plan

1. Consciously notice when shame arises in your child and try to understand its trigger. Then actively try to reduce the shame at the moment by telling the kid that they are good, validating their struggle, and maybe modeling (not telling) the required behavior without lecturing them.

2. Every time your kid does something that you don't like try to be less judgemental about it. Think of the most generous explanation and assume that if you need to. This will help you become more understanding in the long run.

Self-Evaluation

What did you learn about shame and understanding in this chapter? How did the action plan help?

_____

_____

_____

_____

_____

_____

_____

_____

_____

_____

_____

_____

_____

_____

_____

_____

_____

_____

_____

_____

_____

_____

_____

_____

Chapter 9:
Tell the Truth

Chapter Overview

Telling the truth is a foundation of a relationship, even with your kids. It increases their trust in you and in return, they can open up more to you.

Read ahead to understand how truth can be a driving force in a relationship.

Goal Statement

"I will learn to improve my relationship with my kids by sticking to truth in our conversations."

Chapter Summary

Your ability to tell your kids the truth depends on your ability to handle overwhelming emotions during these moments. That is why you must work on yourself too to be better able to help your kids. You might think that the truth would be too hard on kids but with your supporting, honest and caring presence, they won't feel scared. Moreover, they will begin to understand that even the most difficult emotions can be managed.

In your absence and lack of enough information, they will panic. And in their attempt to cope, they will either choose self-blame or self-doubt as a tool as it gives them control over the situation. "I must be a bad child, and if I improve everything will be alright." Or "I must have perceived the situation wrongfully. I cannot trust how I feel about the outer world."

Both of these coping mechanisms are bad for your child. That's why you need clear, direct, and honest communication. Once they start understanding things, regulating their emotions would become easier.

There are four ways for you to ensure this effective communication –

1. Confirming perceptions – Children notice more than they know. They are keen observers. So, whenever anything happens that is out of routine for your kid, you must confirm their perception by repeating exactly what happened. It doesn't matter if the kid displays any discomfort or not. You might want to assure your child that it wasn't his fault. This will help your child to trust his perceptions and stand up for himself as a grown-up.

2. Honoring your child's questions – When your kid asks a question that you believe is too mature for his age, know that they are already thinking about it. You can start honoring their questions with acknowledgment and some truth.

3. Labeling what you don't know – When your kid asks you something and you don't know the answer, simply accept the fact. Your kid doesn't really need the answer, he just needs to feel supported at the moment. Your responding to their question confirms your presence at the moment and that is enough.

4. Focusing on the how – Don't get stuck up on communicating the what of the truth. What matters more is how you communicate it. You can start by preparing your child for what's to come. Eye

contact, pauses, deep breaths, and occasional rub on the back might help you communicate a hard truth better. And when your child reacts to the new information, you should respond with acknowledgment, validation, and permission to feel. This would show your child that struggling with tough emotions is common, but eventually, they will get through.

Check for Understanding

1. Telling the truth to the kids is wrong.

   TRUE   **FALSE**

2. Children don't observe a lot.

   TRUE   **FALSE**

3. Adults should simply deny children's perceptions.

   TRUE   **FALSE**

4. Kind gestures towards kids only serve to make them weak and dependent.

   TRUE   **FALSE**

Reflection Questions

1. Have you ever witnessed your child self-blaming/ self-doubting? Cite some real-life examples.

   _____

   _____

   _____

   _____

_____

_____

_____

2. When your child asks you a difficult question, how do you react? Cite real-life examples.

_____

_____

_____

_____

_____

_____

_____

3. Do you believe in the idea of telling the truth to your children? Why, or why not?

_____

_____

_____

_____

_____

_____

_____

4. How conscious are you of your child's feelings while communicating something to them? What gestures do you use to calm them down?

_____

_____

_____

_____

_____

_____

_____

Action Plan

1. When your child notices something, don't tell them they have noticed it wrong if they haven't. Confirm their perceptions, validate their feelings, and let them talk about it to you.

2. In case there's a truth you believe they are not fully ready for, give them at least something.

3. While communicating the truth, be caring, show your presence, and talk in a non-judgmental manner.

Self-Evaluation

What new did you learn about telling the truth in this chapter? How much help was the action plan?

_____

_____

_____

_____

_____

Chapter 10:
Self-Care

Chapter Overview

The chapter is about how self-care is really important for you as a parent. Everyone has needs and no one can sacrifice them all the time. If you do that as a parent, you will eventually wear down, and become resentful of your kid.

Read ahead to understand why self-care is so important in parenting.

Goal Statement

"I will learn to adopt self-care by acknowledging my own needs."

Chapter Summary

Parenthood means helping your child while also growing yourself. If you don't take care of your own needs, you become depleted and resentful. It doesn't help you and it doesn't help your kids who start blaming themselves for your depleted state. So, you must take care of yourselves too. That's hard for parents who worry a lot about being selfish. Their guilt exacerbates in case their child protests. Yet you as a parent must set firm boundaries to ensure that you take care of yourself. Your kid will actually feel comforted as they'll appreciate your sturdiness and self-assurance in you.

When you shift to self-care mode, there will be discomfort marking your progress. But that's okay.

Here's a list of self-care strategies that you can follow –

1. **Breathing** – Deep breathing is the key that unlocks the room where all other coping strategies live. It regulates several important bodily processes that eventually trigger your calming-down process and help you handle life situations better.

2. **Acknowledge, Validate, Permit (AVP)** – Acknowledge your feelings by labeling them, validate them by accepting them as true, and permit them to exist.

3. **Getting your needs met and tolerating stress** – The only way to get your needs met is to simultaneously tolerate others' distress. It's not your job to ensure someone else is happy.

4. **One thing for myself** – If self-care feels hard, start with one thing that you can do for yourself. It means making and keeping promises to yourself.

5. **Repair with yourself** – Self-care involves getting good at repairing with yourself while repairing well with others.

Check for Understanding

1. Sacrificing all your needs is quintessential to being a good parent.

   TRUE   **FALSE**

2. Your child's needs are more important than yours.

   TRUE   **FALSE**

3. You should acknowledge & validate your own feelings too.

   TRUE   **FALSE**

4. Self-care is key to being a good parent.

   TRUE   **FALSE**

Reflection Questions

1. What are your unmet needs as a parent?

_____

_____

_____

_____

_____

_____

_____

2. When your and your kid's need collide, what do you do?

_____

_____

_____

_____

_____

_____

3. How much important is your personal growth in your life? How is being a parent affecting that?

_____

_____

_____

_____

_____

_____

_____

Action Plan

1. If you struggle with self-care, start with self-compassion.

2. Refer to the **How to do It** sections of all the self-care strategies from the original book.

3. Repeat to yourself aloud "I am allowed to have things for myself even if they inconvenience others." Notice how your body reacts to this statement. If it feels bad, it means that you might not be taking care of your own needs. Keep repeating the mantra & acting on it, until the feeling disappears.

4. Learn to say no to things and establish firm boundaries.

Self-Evaluation

What did learn about the impact of self-care on your parenting style? Did the action plan help you take better care of yourself?

_____

_____

_____

_____

_____

Chapter 11:
Build Connection Capital

Chapter Overview

This chapter talks about how connection capital is essential in your relationship with your kids. With enough of this capital, you can ask them to do things that they might otherwise not be willing to do. The chapter also gives you the ways that you can use to build the connection capital.

Goal Statement

"I will learn to effect behavior change in my kid by building connection capital."

Chapter Summary

You cannot change your kid's behavior until you build a connection with them. So, you need to orient your efforts towards connection. If they don't feel connected to you or if they feel alone with a problem, their connection capital depletes and that shows in their behavior. Contrarily, having a good amount of connection capital makes them feel confident, capable, safe, and worthy, and it shows in their behavior as well. Remember that this capital flows in two ways. It gets filled when you build connections and gets depleted when you ask your kids to do something they don't want to. The key is to ensure that you never run out of it.

Here are some strategies that you can use.

1. Play No Phone (PNP) Time – You can set aside a proper time slot where your kid gets your full undivided attention. You put all your electronic gadgets away for this period. It only needs you to enter your child's world for 10-15 minutes. Ensure that you don't ask questions during this time. Instead, describe what your kid's doing, mimic them, and practice reflective listening.

2. The Fill-up game – The author believes that children behave badly when they don't have enough of their parents. To overcome that, she suggests the fill-up game.

3. Emotional vaccination – Vaccination prepares us for future threats. Similarly, with emotional vaccination, you connect with your children before a big-feelings moment. You connect, validate the challenge that they might soon be facing, and verbalize or even rehearse how they can handle it. This way, your child becomes more equipped to handle it.

4. The Feeling Bench – Feelings are scary when you are alone in them. When your child is having a hard time, make sure to sit with them on the feeling bench.

5. Playfulness – Silliness, and playfulness are amazing connection capital builders that you can use to build a better connection with your child.

6. "Did I ever tell you about the time…?" – In this approach, you relate to your child's struggle through a personal experience. You tell them a story that tells them that they are not alone to struggle, that they are

a good kid having a hard time. Not only that, when you tell them your problem, they are better able to access their own problem solver.

7. Change the ending – Everyone messes up in their relationships but if you learn to repair, you get the opportunity to change the ending of the story. Your child will remember the incident from a different perspective when you repair it than when you do not. A repair goes further than an apology. It involves an apology but that's not its entirety.

Check for Understanding

1. Parents should give enough time and attention to their kids to build connection capital.

   TRUE   **FALSE**

2. The playfulness with kids is an impactful way of building connection capital.

   TRUE   **FALSE**

3. Emotionally preparing kids for a big moment is a waste of time.

   TRUE   **FALSE**

4. It should be the child's responsibility to repair with the parent.

   TRUE   **FALSE**

Reflection Questions

1. Do you prepare your kids for emotionally challenging moments? Why or why not?

_____

_____

_____

_____

_____

_____

_____

2. How playful are you with your kids? What does playfulness add to the relationship?

_____

_____

_____

_____

_____

_____

_____

3. Do you share your life stories with your kids? What kind of stories do you share and why?

_____

_____

_____

_____

_____

_____

_____

4. How much connection capital do you think you have with your kid?
   Is it enough to conform to your demands?

_____

_____

_____

_____

_____

_____

_____

Action Plan

1. Start with the connection. Behavior comes last.
2. Refer to the original book for the scripts to implement the connection strategies with your kids.
3. Don't judge your kid for their feelings. Rather, make them feel understood.
4. Have some playtime with your kids where they can be as creative as they want to be.

Self-Evaluation

What new did you learn about building connection capital in this chapter? How did the action plan help you?

_____

_____

_____

_____

_____

_____

_____

_____

_____

_____

_____

_____

_____

_____

_____

_____

_____

_____

_____

_____

_____

_____

Chapter 12:
Not Listening

Chapter Overview

This chapter talks about how your child not listening to you is a relationship problem that needs to be addressed accordingly. The chapter also gives you a few techniques to connect better with your kid to make them listen to you.

Read ahead to understand how not listening to you is a manifestation of a gap in connection.

Goal statement

"I will learn to address the not listening to me issue of my kid by improving our connection."

Chapter Summary

The more connected we feel to someone, the more likely we are to comply with their requests. So, if your child is not listening to you, it's a relationship problem. And it's not only you, all parent-child relationships need extra love and attention sometimes. The second element to this listening problem is the parents always ask kids to stop something they enjoy to do something that they don't. If you infuse connection, respect, playfulness, and trust in your relationship with your kid.

Here are a few strategies that you can use to address the listening problem –

1. **Connect before you ask** – It's essential that you connect with your kids outside the moments that you need them to cooperate. It will make them more likely to comply with your requests.

2. **Give your child a choice** – If you give your kids a choice, it makes them more likely to cooperate. Ensure that the choices you offer are the ones that you are comfortable with.

3. **Humor** – When you introduce playfulness and humor in your relationship with your kids, your connection with your kid improves making them more likely to cooperate with you.

4. **Close your eyes hack** – When you ask your kid to do something while you place your hands on your eyes, you infuse respect, trust, independence, control, and playfulness all at once. When kids feel that, they are more likely to comply. This strategy can be applied to older kids too by using the fundamental ideas from this strategy, i.e., to demonstrate trust, respect, independence, control, and playfulness.

5. **Role-Reversal Game** – In this game, instead of your kid listening to you, you have to listen to what your kid says given it's safe and sound. It helps you connect with your child through playfulness.

Check for Understanding

1. You should only ask your kid to do what they enjoy doing.
   TRUE   **FALSE**

2. Giving your child a choice makes you a less effective parent.
   TRUE   **FALSE**

3. Humor improves your relationship with kids.

   TRUE   **FALSE**

4. Showing trust in your kids leads them to break it.

   TRUE   **FALSE**

Reflection Questions

1. Does your child listen to you? Why, or why not?

_____

_____

_____

_____

_____

_____

_____

2. Do you trust your child? Does your child know it through your actions?

_____

_____

_____

_____

_____

_____

_____

3. Who's that one person who always gets along well with all children? What are their traits?

_____

_____

_____

_____

_____

_____

4. What do you think the role-reversal game can help you achieve?

_____

_____

_____

_____

_____

_____

Action Plan

1. Make it a point to connect with your child outside the moments that you need them to cooperate with you.
2. Bring them to the decision table by giving them a choice between two things. Make sure that both choices are acceptable to you.
3. Show them in different ways that you trust them.

Self-Evaluation

What new did you learn in this chapter? How much help was the action plan?

_____

_____

_____

_____

_____

_____

_____

_____

_____

_____

_____

_____

_____

_____

_____

_____

_____

_____

_____

_____

_____

_____

Chapter 13:
Emotional Tantrums

Chapter Overview

This chapter explains the significance of emotional tantrums. It talks about how tantrums are not just normal, but healthy as well. It's an expression of a child's helplessness when they want something but cannot have it. It's healthy as it demonstrates that the kid recognizes their needs.

Read ahead to understand the reason behind emotional tantrums.

Goal Statement

"I will learn to tackle my child's tantrums by adopting the strategies listed in this chapter."

Chapter Summary

Tantrums are not just normal, they are healthy. They only show that a child cannot manage the emotional demands of a situation. It's a biological state of dysregulation when your child wants something but cannot have it. But your primary goal shouldn't be to end it.

You want your kids to want for themselves, to be able to recognize and assert their desires. But that will not happen if you teach them only subservience and compliance as kids. You must recognize that it's just a human being expressing feelings of being overwhelmed when not having their desires met. If you just make them feel seen, safe, and understood, that's all they need at that moment.

Here are the strategies that can help you while your child is having a tantrum –

1. **Remind yourself of your own goodness** – External blame has the tendency to inspire internal blame. So, remind yourself that there is nothing wrong with your kid, and there's nothing wrong with your kid.

2. **Two things are true** – The idea is that you have to make decisions and your kids are allowed to have and express their feelings. This needs to be conveyed with permission and empathy.

3. **Name the wish** - Name the wish underneath a child's meltdown as it makes them feel seen while letting you connect and empathize with them.

4. **Validate the Magnitude** – Validating the magnitude of your kid is just as essential to make them feel seen. This helps your kid to better articulate the extent of their feelings.

Check for Understanding

1. Your child shouldn't have any emotional tantrums at all.
   TRUE   **FALSE**

2. Tantrums signify that your kid can't meet their needs.
   TRUE   **FALSE**

3. You should immediately put an end to your kid's tantrum.
   TRUE   **FALSE**

4. It eases your kid's emotional pain if you make them feel seen.

   TRUE   **FALSE**

Reflection Questions

1. What sort of tantrums does your child resort to? Cite real-life examples.

_____

_____

_____

_____

_____

_____

_____

2. As an adult, do you also have moments of emotional tantrums? Elaborate.

_____

_____

_____

_____

_____

_____

_____

3. What is the most successful strategy for tackling your child's emotional tantrums that you have used? Elaborate.

_____

_____

_____

_____

_____

_____

_____

4. What are the triggers of your child's emotional tantrums? Cite examples from your experience.

_____

_____

_____

_____

_____

_____

_____

Action Plan

1. Don't take the bait when your kid is having a tantrum.
2. Even when your kid is having a tantrum, don't mend any boundaries just to let them have their way.
3. Make it a point to communicate that you notice the magnitude of your child's emotions. This would make them feel seen.

Self-Evaluation

What new did you learn about emotional tantrums in this chapter? How did the action plan help you?

_____

_____

_____

_____

_____

_____

_____

_____

_____

_____

_____

_____

_____

_____

_____

_____

_____

_____

_____

_____

_____

Chapter 14:
Aggressive Tantrums
(Hitting, Biting, Throwing)

Chapter Overview

This chapter explains how even aggressive tantrums are perfectly normal, and healthy. Children's brain isn't fully developed at a very young age. In those years, they are more inclined towards aggressive tantrums. The chapter talks about how you can give a safe environment for your kids to express themselves.

Read ahead to know how you should handle your kids' aggressive tantrums.

Goal Statement

"I will learn to let my kid express their aggressive tantrums by providing them a safe environment."

Chapter Summary

The prefrontal cortex is responsible for language, forward-thinking, perspective, and other executive functions in an individual. In children, this part is underdeveloped. That's why they indulge in aggressive tantrums from time to time. To learn to control these urges is a part of their development process and thus is completely normal. Kids need their parents to help them stay grounded by embodying authority.

But a lot of adults struggle with that and expect kids to be responsible for themselves.

Once you can embody authority, you get the ability to keep your own body calm and to keep your kid safe. In explosive tantrum moments, you shouldn't focus on lecturing and correcting your kid, containment should be your only goal.

Here are the strategies that you can follow to handle your kid's aggressive tantrums –

1. **"I Won't Let You"** - Say this aloud when your kid is involved in an aggressive tantrum like hitting, biting, etc. It communicates that the parent is in charge. When a kid cannot make good decisions, they need an adult to provide the containment.

2. **Differentiate urge from action** - Having the urge to bite or hit is okay but doing that to someone is not. You must communicate that to your kid. That's why it is suggested to bring your child to a safe space to let them discharge their tantrums.

3. **Contain the Fire** - Your goal isn't to extinguish the emotional fire of your kids but to contain it. Keep that in mind while dealing with them.

4. **Personify the Feelings** - When you personify your kid's feelings and believe that their unkind words are directed at their feelings and not yours, it helps you to stay grounded and calm in the situation.

5. **Telling the story** - By telling the story of the incident, you return to the scene of the emotional fire and review the chaotic meltdown moment to build coherence. This simple act of adding your presence, coherence, and a narrative will change how the experience gets stored in the child's body.

Check for Understanding

1. Aggressive tantrums are not normal for kids.

   TRUE　　　　**FALSE**

2. You should let your kid express their tantrums even if that means hurting others in the process.

   TRUE　　　　**FALSE**

3. Your goal should always be to extinguish the emotional fire of your kid.

   TRUE　　　　**FALSE**

4. You should distance yourself from your kid as a punishment for them for their aggressive behavior.

   TRUE　　　　**FALSE**

Reflection Questions

1. Do your kids display aggressive tantrums? How do you handle the situation?

_____

_____

_____

_____

_____

_____

_____

2. When your kid says unkind things to you, how does that make you
   feel and react?

   _____

   _____

   _____

   _____

   _____

   _____

   _____

3. How important do you think it is to be an authoritative figure for your
   kids?

   _____

   _____

   _____

   _____

   _____

   _____

   _____

Action Plan

1. During an aggressive tantrum, try applying the strategies to handle the situation. Apply Contain the fire strategy from the original book.

2. Whenever your kid is indulged in aggressive behavior, step in to let them know that you are in control and you won't let them hurt anybody, including themselves.

3. It's healthy if your kid can verbally express their aggressive desire, "I feel like I need to kick someone." In that case bring them to a safe environment, where they can vent their anger without hurting themselves or anybody else.

Self-Evaluation

What new did you learn in this chapter? Did the action plan help you handle your kid's aggressive tantrums?

_____

_____

_____

_____

_____

_____

_____

_____

_____

_____

_____

Chapter 15:
Sibling Rivalry

Chapter Overview

The chapter explains sibling rivalry in detail. Sibling rivalry isn't just about childish fights and kids not liking each other. Below the surface, there are different fears that eventually manifest in their behavior.

Read ahead to understand more about sibling rivalry.

Goal Statement

"I will learn to control sibling rivalry by putting my kids at ease."

Chapter Summary

In the older child, siblinghood activates attachment needs and abandonment fears. Giving them special time can help them feel more secure in their relationship with their parents. You must accept that your kids have a range of feelings about their siblings and you must teach them how to regulate those feelings. It's not our feelings that are the problem, it's not being able to regulate them that creates harmful results. The more you connect with your kids on their feelings, the better they can regulate their emotions.

Even the order of the birth is a very essential factor when talking about feelings. Like, the firstborns are wired for the full attention of their parents. Having a new sibling completely changes the dynamics of their world.

Here are a few strategies that you can use to address sibling rivalry –

1. **PNP Time** - When each child gets dedicated alone time to spend with a parent, it serves to reduce sibling rivalry.

2. **"We Don't Do Fair, We Do Individual Needs"** - When parents get stuck on being fair, one kid gets whatever the other one is. It means that at any time, one sibling is looking at the other to define their own needs. But we want to orient our kids inward to figure out their own needs instead of looking at others. Otherwise, they will grow into adults who look at others to figure out what they need in life.

3. **Allow Venting (But only to you)** - You should establish with your kids that it is okay to talk to you, and only you, about any feelings they have for their siblings. In this way, those feelings won't show up in their behavior.

4. **Step in when there's danger; slow down and narrate when there's not** - If your kid's agitated and it is an imminently dangerous situation, you have to step in to resolve the situation as soon as possible. But in situations that aren't dangerous, you can use the opportunity to teach your kids to slow down and solve their problems themselves.

Check for Understanding

1. When each child gets special attention from their parents, it serves to ease sibling rivalry.

   TRUE   **FALSE**

2. You should prioritize individual needs instead of trying to be fair.

   TRUE   **FALSE**

3. You should allow your kid to vent their feelings only to you.

   TRUE   **FALSE**

4. Firstborns are wired for the full attention of their parents.

   TRUE   **FALSE**

Reflection Questions

1. What is the relationship between your kids like? Elaborate.

_____

_____

_____

_____

_____

_____

_____

2. Is there a pattern to your kids' conflict? Cite some real-life examples.

_____

_____

_____

_____

_____

_____

_____

3. How do you currently manage the sibling rivalry among your kids?

_____

_____

_____

_____

_____

_____

_____

4. Do your kids come to you expressing their feelings about their siblings? How does it go?

_____

_____

_____

_____

_____

_____

_____

Action Plan

1. Give more special time and attention to your kids separately.
2. Acknowledge, validate, and permit your kid's feelings in difficult situations.

Self-Evaluation

What new did you learn about sibling rivalry in this chapter? Did the action plan prove helpful?

_____

_____

_____

_____

_____

_____

_____

_____

_____

_____

_____

_____

_____

_____

_____

_____

_____

_____

_____

_____

Chapter 16:
Rudeness and Defiance

Chapter Overview

The chapter talks about what rudeness & defiance from your kid means and what it doesn't. According to the author, it is a sign of emotional dysregulation that your kid is going through. And when you as a parent react to it aggressively, it only makes the situation worse. Read ahead to understand defiant behavior in detail.

Goal Statement

"I will learn to understand my kid's defiant behavior by not being reactive towards it."

Chapter Summary

When your kid is being rude or defiant, you can either view it as a sign of disrespect towards you or you can view it in terms of emotional dysregulation that your child is going through. It happens to adults as well when they feel misunderstood when they have a desire to feel seen and they don't. But instead of understanding that, you are more likely to assert yourself through punishment.

A child's rudeness when met with a parent's reactivity makes the child feel even more misunderstood and alone. It exacerbates their feelings leading to more dysregulation. Thus, you must see your child's rude words as a desperate plea for help. Once you meet their rudeness with empathy and kindness, it will make them feel seen.

Here are the strategies that you can follow to tackle your child's rudeness and defiance

1. **Don't take the bait** - Your child's on-the-surface behavior is a sign that something deeper and more vulnerable is inside them. Seeing what lies underneath the words means that you are not taking the bait and reacting to their rude behavior with anger. It involves putting a firm boundary around your child's behavior and then providing a generous interpretation of their behavior.

2. **Embody your authority** - You must do this without resorting to scares and punishments. Establish boundaries and narrate the reason behind doing so. See if you can help your child express their feelings without violating the boundary. Help your kid with impulse control once things are calmer.

3. **State the truth** - When you are making a rule that you know that your child won't like, state the truth. It will help you build a connection by validating their experience.

4. **Connect and build regulation when things are calm** - When the situation is charged, it is unlikely for you to be able to build a connection at that moment. Thus, it is better that you connect with your kid when things are calm.

Check for Understanding

1. You shouldn't react aggressively to your kid's rude behavior.
   TRUE   **FALSE**

2. Stating the truth to your child worsens your relationship with them.
   TRUE   **FALSE**

3. Your child should violate their boundaries every now and then.

   TRUE   **FALSE**

4. It is easier to connect with your child when things are calm.

   TRUE   **FALSE**

Reflection Questions

1. How often does your child act rude & defiant? When does it usually happy?

   _____

   _____

   _____

   _____

   _____

   _____

2. How do you handle the moments of rudeness & defiance from your child?

   _____

   _____

   _____

   _____

   _____

   _____

3. When do you, as an adult, behave rudely with others? What leads you to do it?

_____

_____

_____

_____

_____

_____

4. 'When shown empathy, the child feels seen and the rudeness disappears gradually' – Do you agree with this statement? Why, or why not?

_____

_____

_____

_____

_____

_____

Action Plan

1. When your child is being rude, don't react with anger. Instead, empathize and be curious about their struggle.

2. Know that It is a moment of dysregulation for your kid, and not disrespect towards you that's leading them to do so.

3. Be truthful to your kids and validate their hard experiences. They will feel seen that way.

Self-Evaluation

What did you get to learn about rudeness and defiance in this chapter? Did the action plan help you?

_____

_____

_____

_____

_____

_____

_____

_____

_____

_____

_____

_____

_____

_____

_____

Chapter 17:
Whining

Chapter Overview

This chapter talks about how kids whining might look like ungratefulness, it is much more than that. Whining happens when there's a strong desire along with a feeling of powerlessness. Or they might whine when they feel alone and in need of a connection.

Read ahead to understand how you can help your whining kid with empathy.

Goal Statement

"I will learn to manage the whining of my kid by following the mentioned strategies."

Chapter Summary

To parents, kids' whining looks like ungratefulness. But that is not really the case. Whining drives strength from a combination of strong desire and powerlessness. And if whining represents powerlessness, it might trigger you if your parents taught you to not show any vulnerability.

Kids also whine when they feel alone and are looking for a connection. So, even when you define boundaries for a whining kid, you can still practice understanding and connecting. You still don't have to change your decision. When they are whining, children just need to let it all out and you should simply let them do it.

Here are a few strategies for you to manage your kid's whining

1. **Embrace your inner whiner** - Even for adults, wanting and not having is a brutal experience. And they often whine about it. Once you embrace that whiner inside you, your kid's whining will bother you a lot less.

2. **Humor** - You can offer your kid connection and hopefulness by responding to their whining with humor. Remember to not mock or insult them.

3. **Restate the request in your own voice** - When your kid makes a whining request, model the request for them in your own strong voice and move on instead of lecturing them. Trust your child to learn the lesson.

4. **See the Need** - When your kids whine, they are asking for more attention, warmth, empathy, and validation. You need to acknowledge, validate, and fulfill the need.

Check for Understanding

1. You shouldn't ever let your kid whine.

   TRUE   **FALSE**

2. Your boundaries need not change just because your kid is whining.

   TRUE   **FALSE**

3. Whining is a symptom of a deeper need.

   TRUE   **FALSE**

4. One should never show vulnerability.

   TRUE   **FALSE**

Reflection Questions

1. What's your current strategy to manage a whining kid?

_____

_____

_____

_____

_____

_____

2. *"Whining means there's a deeper need"* – What do you understand from this statement?

_____

_____

_____

_____

_____

_____

3. What makes you whine as an adult? Cite some real-life examples.

_____

_____

_____

_____

_____

_____

4. Was it okay in your childhood to show vulnerability? How did your
   parents react to that?

_____

_____

_____

_____

_____

_____

_____

Action Plan

1. Practice whining in front of the mirror in order to embrace the whiner
   inside of you. This will make you less judgemental of your kid's
   whining.
2. Always try to look deeper into your child's behavior.
3. Make humor your go-to tool for parenting.

Self-Evaluation

What new did you learn in this chapter? Did the action plan help you with your kid's whining?

_____

_____

_____

_____

_____

_____

_____

_____

_____

_____

_____

_____

_____

_____

_____

_____

_____

_____

_____

_____

_____

Chapter 18:
Lying

Chapter overview

This chapter addresses the lying problem that kids often develop. Instead of seeing it as your kid getting out of your hands, lying signifies that there is something that makes it hard for your kid to trust you with the truth. It then becomes your responsibility to bridge that gap.

Read ahead to understand why your kid lies to you.

Goal statement

"I will learn to build trust with my kid by working on our relationship."

Chapter Summary

There are a few reasons that your kid might lie to you. First, the line between fantasy and reality is murkier for them than for adults. They often engage in pretend play to explore their issues. So, to cope with their guilt or in the fear of disappointing you, they might enter their fantasy world, which might sound like a lie to you. In reality, it is their wish that they are expressing. It is a sign of their need to feel safe & good inside.

Your child's survival depends on their attachment to you and if they believe that the truth will threaten that attachment, they are likely to lie. It isn't manipulation, it's self-defense.

Another scenario when children might lie is to assert their independence when they feel too controlled by their parents. As human beings, we hate being controlled. The same goes for the kids for whom lying becomes a core strategy to ensure this basic human need for themselves.

When dealing with kids who lie often, your goal should be to increase truth-telling in the future rather than increase confessions now. They will start telling you the truth once they see you as a safe adult who can handle all of their experiences.

Here are a few strategies that you can follow –

1. **Reframe the lie as a wish** - See your kid's lie as a wish and it will allow you to be on the same team as your child.

2. **Wait and provide an opening later** - When your kid is defending a lie, it won't serve anyone to confront them. First work on reducing shame to make the change possible later.

3. **"If it did happen" approach** - It's effective to share it with your kid how you would respond if the kid shared the truth. It makes them realize that it is safe for them to share the truth with you.

4. **Asking a child what he needs to be honest with you** - It is helpful if you connect with the child outside the moment of lying. You could ask them for the things they might need from you in order to trust you with the truth.

Check for Understanding

1. Children often lie as a survival mechanism.

   TRUE   **FALSE**

2. Lying might be a symptom of shame.

   TRUE   **FALSE**

3. A child might lie when they have too much freedom.

   TRUE   **FALSE**

4. Lying means your kid is a bad kid.

   TRUE   **FALSE**

5. Your end goal should be to get your child to confess.

   TRUE   **FALSE**

Reflection Questions

1. Do you think your child has a lying problem? Cite real-life examples.

_____

_____

_____

_____

_____

_____

_____

2. How do you handle your lying children? Cite real-life examples.

_____

_____

_____

_____

_____

_____

_____

3. Do you think you provide a safe environment for your kid to tell you the truth? Elaborate.

_____

_____

_____

_____

_____

_____

4. Who takes most of the decisions for your kids? If it's you, do you tend to micro-manage?

_____

_____

_____

_____

_____

_____

Action Plan

1. Make it a point to demonstrate in all situations that you trust your kid. Sometimes trusting is more important than understanding.
2. Always try to bring the shame down by being less judgmental of your kid.

3. Don't react aggressively whenever your child makes a mistake. It will only serve to make them hide things from you.

4. Tell them about the times when you made a mistake but your parents helped you solve the issue. Make them see that it is normal to do things you are not always proud of.

Self-Evaluation

What new did you learn about your kid's lying habit? Did the action plan help you in building trust with your kid?

_____

_____

_____

_____

_____

_____

_____

_____

_____

_____

_____

_____

_____

_____

_____

_____

_____

Are you enjoying the book so far?

If so, please help us reach more readers by taking 30 seconds to write just a few words on Amazon by using the QR code below

Or, you can choose to leave one later...

Scan me

Chapter 19:
Fears and Anxiety

Chapter overview

The chapter talks about the times when your kid is feeling any fear or anxiety. While the normal strategy is to tackle such a situation with logic, it doesn't work. Instead, your kid needs your presence to feel safe again.

Read ahead to understand how you can be there for your kid when they are scared and anxious.

Goal Statement

"I will learn to help my kid with their fears by being present for them."

Chapter Summary

When kids feel fearful and anxious, they need your help to feel safe again. While you might try to tell them why they shouldn't feel panicky, it's never a successful strategy. Instead, they need your presence and connection, instead of logic to feel safe. It's their aloneness in fear that is the scariest part.

When you try to talk them out of their fears and anxiety, they start to believe that it's wrong for them to feel that way. They start having anxiety about anxiety. The only way to handle it effectively is to increase tolerance for it.

Here are a few strategies that you can use with your kid to help them manage their fears and anxiety.

1. **Jump into the hole with them** - The hole represents their anxiety. Instead of trying to pull them out of it, jump into it with them. When you do that, you communicate that it is okay to be anxious about something. By joining them, you tell them that the feeling isn't quite overwhelming for an adult.

2. **Dry runs** - Parents don't want to bring up situations that make their kids anxious. But avoidance is only going to increase anxiety. It tells your child that you are also anxious about that thing and thus, don't want to talk about it. Dry runs are the opposite of avoidance. You willingly rehearse for difficult situations with your kids. It prepares them for when the real thing happens.

3. **Script for addressing specific fears** - Talk to your child about their fears. This is an exercise aimed at collecting more information about their fears. The next step is to validate your child's fear. Tell them that their fears make sense. At this stage, it is essential to communicate to them that communication is important and that you are glad that they talked to you about it. Then, engage your child to solve the problem with you. Lead them, but don't solve it for them.

Check for Understanding

1. When kids feel scared, they are looking for a logical explanation.

    TRUE   **FALSE**

2. You should never validate your child's fears.

    TRUE   **FALSE**

3. Dry runs are unimportant in addressing your kid's anxiety.

    TRUE   **FALSE**

4. You should mandate your kids to shut down vulnerability.

    TRUE   **FALSE**

Reflection Questions

1. What is your current strategy to manage your kid's fears & anxiety? Elaborate.

    _____

    _____

    _____

    _____

    _____

    _____

    _____

2. Do you judge your kid for their fears and anxiety? Elaborate.

    _____

    _____

    _____

    _____

    _____

_____

_____

3. Have you ever tried to share your fears as a kid with your child to validate their experience? Cite some real-life examples.

_____

_____

_____

_____

_____

_____

Action Plan

1. Whenever your kid's scared, ask them "There must be something to this, tell me more."

2. Don't try to talk them out of their fear, because eventually, you want them to be able to trust their intuitions.

3. To jump into the hole with them, you must validate your child's fear and provide them with your genuine presence.

Self-Evaluation

What new did this chapter teach you? Did you find the action plan helpful?

_____

_____

_____

_____

_____

_____

_____

_____

_____

_____

_____

_____

_____

_____

_____

_____

_____

_____

_____

_____

_____

_____

_____

Chapter 20:
Hesitation and Shyness

Chapter Overview

The chapter talks about the reasons behind your child's hesitance and anxiety, and how you can work on addressing it with them. Everything that you perceive as hesitance might not be it. Blindly rushing is not what confidence is. If your kid knows what they need and stick by it, even not doing something can be a sign of confidence.

Read ahead to understand more about your kid's hesitation and shyness.

Goal Statement

"I will try to understand my kid's hesitance by being less reactive and more curious."

Chapter Summary

Hesitation and shyness are not problems to fix. But when kids behave this way, it makes parents more anxious than their kids. That's why they rush in to fix it. But you need a better understanding to help your kids. If you start thinking "he will be like this forever", this creates a self-fulfilling cycle. A child often comes to internalize their parent's judgment, intensifying their hesitance and anxiety.

While parents see confidence as a counter to their kids' hesitancy, they often feel to understand the definition of confidence. Confidence isn't necessarily joining a group or engaging in activity right away. It isn't being ready – it's knowing when you're ready.

Here are a few strategies that you can use to help your kid with their hesitation and shyness –

1. **Check-in with yourself** - You might be getting very triggered by your child's shyness, especially if you are outgoing. Knowing your own trigger will help you separate your experience from your child's.

2. **Validate + "You'll know when you are ready"** - Even if you don't understand, know that your child's hesitation comes from a real place. Validate it and assure them that they will know when they are ready.

3. **Preparation** - Prepare with your kids for what's to come. It makes them better handle the situations that otherwise frighten them.

4. **Avoid labeling** - Don't label your child as something because they respond to the versions of themselves that you reflect. Such rigidity makes growth difficult.

Check for Understanding

1. Your child's shyness is a big problem that can only be solved with medications.

   TRUE   **FALSE**

2. Children often come to internalize parental judgments.

   TRUE   **FALSE**

3. Validating your child's hesitation increases their self-trust.

   TRUE   **FALSE**

4. Labeling your child stimulates their growth.

   TRUE   **FALSE**

Reflection Questions

1. Do you think your child is hesitant/shy? Cite real-life examples.

_____

_____

_____

_____

_____

_____

_____

2. What do you understand by confidence? According to you, how does
   it manifest in a child's behavior?

_____

_____

_____

_____

_____

_____

3. Do you often judge or label your child instead of understanding their
   point of view? Justify by citing real-life examples.

_____

_____

_____

_____

_____

_____

_____

4. Do you get triggered when your child behaves hesitantly? How do you react? Do you think it's the best way to go about it?

_____

_____

_____

_____

_____

_____

_____

Action Plan

1. Tell your child often "You'll know when you're ready". Self-trust is the essence of confidence.

2. You might want to give your child a break from larger social gatherings and work things out with them, by telling them how they are not alone in such anxieties.

Self-Evaluation

What new did you learn about hesitation and shyness in this chapter? Did the action plan help you manage your kid's shyness?

_____

_____

_____

_____

_____

_____

_____

_____

_____

_____

_____

_____

_____

_____

_____

_____

_____

_____

_____

_____

_____

_____

_____

_____

Chapter 21:
Frustration Intolerance

Chapter Overview

The chapter talks about how frustration is something that cannot be avoided in life. Whenever you struggle with something, frustration builds up inside you. In such a scenario, you must learn to tolerate it so that you don't give up everything that feels challenging. This makes frustration tolerance a key skill for your kid to achieve great things in life.

Read ahead to understand how frustration intolerance might be affecting your kid.

Goal Statement

"I will help my kid build frustration tolerance by adopting the growth mindset."

Chapter Summary

The more we embrace mistakes and struggles, the more we set the stage for growth, success, and achievement. Tolerating frustration is key to managing disappointments, communicating effectively, and sticking with personal goals. For your kids to develop a tolerance for their frustration, you must develop a tolerance for their frustration. The more you are okay with struggling with a challenge, the more your kid will be okay with it.

The growth mindset with the belief that abilities can be cultivated through effort and persistence creates a pathway to learning. It can help both an adult and a kid stick longer with hard things. It builds tolerance for learning. You have to think in terms of building coping skills instead of skills to find success.

Check for Understanding

1. A growth mindset prioritizes talent over hard work and persistence.

   TRUE   **FALSE**

2. Your kids should be frustration intolerant.

   TRUE   **FALSE**

3. Your reaction to your kids' struggles is a key determinant in their frustration tolerance levels.

   TRUE   **FALSE**

Reflection Questions

1. Do you think your child gives up easily in the face of challenges? Justify with examples.

   _____

   _____

   _____

   _____

   _____

   _____

   _____

2. What is your reaction to your child's struggles? Do you show frustration? Do you encourage them to keep at it or just ask them to leave it?

_____

_____

_____

_____

_____

_____

_____

3. What is your perspective on mistakes? Elaborate.

_____

_____

_____

_____

_____

_____

_____

4. Do you know someone with a growth mindset? Which of their qualities would you like to have? Why?

_____

_____

_____

_____

_____

Action Plan

1. When your kids are performing difficult tasks, be sure to focus on the effort, rather than the outcome.

2. Surround your kids with philosophies & quotes of the growth mindset. You can write things like – "In our family, we love to be challenged." You can refer to the original book for more such quotes that the author uses. You don't need to copy as you can set your own family values

3. Encourage Emotional Vaccination, Dry runs, and "Did I ever tell you about the time?"

Self-Evaluation

What new did you learn about frustration intolerance in this chapter? Did the action plan prove useful?

Chapter 22:
Food and Eating Habits

Chapter Overview

The chapter discusses the food habit challenges that you might face with your kid. While it might cause a lot of anxiety for you as a parent, the best way to go about it for the author is to divide responsibilities. While you decide what gets served, your kid should decide how much to eat.

Read ahead to understand your kid's food and eating challenges in detail.

Goal Statement

"I will learn to ease the anxiety around food habits by adopting a division of responsibility around eating."

Chapter Summary

Kids' eating habits can cause a lot of anxiety for parents. It represents a parent's ability to sustain their kids and fill them up with what they need to thrive in life. It acts as a barometer of how good care are you taking off your kid. Food interactions touch on issues like body sovereignty, and who can make decisions about the same. Once both the parent and the kid turn defensive, the power struggle intensifies.

Adopting Ellyn Satter's division of Responsibility around eating can allow for the development of healthy eating patterns, self-regulation self-confidence, and consent, among other things. It makes parents feel good about their role in their child's eating decisions.

Here are a few strategies to help you with your kid's eating habits –

1. **Mantra** - Having a mantra to guide and keep you grounded is an effective way for you to handle anxiety.

2. **Explain roles** - When you use Satter's division of responsibility, it also becomes your task to let your kid know what they are and aren't in charge of.

3. **Desert-specific strategies** - You have to strategize dessert in a way that it doesn't replace the full meal. Also, it shouldn't be projected as a prize to be coveted.

4. **Snack-specific strategies** - It's you who get to make these decisions according to your needs & perceptions. The only thing you must ensure is that you announce the change and let your kids have their feelings and reactions.

5. **Be ready for the pushback** - In parenting in general, you'll make hard decisions, and your kids will push back. You must learn to handle your kid who's not happy with you. The original book lists a few scripts that you can refer to for this.

Check for Understanding

1. Your children should have no say in their food habits.

    TRUE   **FALSE**

2. Adopting mantras can help you manage your anxieties.

   TRUE   **FALSE**

3. Dividing responsibility around eating can help your kid develop healthy eating patterns.

   TRUE   **FALSE**

4. Your kids shouldn't be allowed to be upset about your decisions.

   TRUE   **FALSE**

Reflection Questions

1. What are your concerns about your kid's eating habits? Elaborate.

   _____

   _____

   _____

   _____

   _____

   _____

   _____

2. How do you currently manage your kid who's not eating as per your expectations?

   _____

   _____

   _____

   _____

   _____

   _____

   _____

3. Do you think diving responsibilities is a good strategy moving forward? Why, or why not?

_____

_____

_____

_____

_____

_____

4. What is the general perspective around snacks and desserts in your family? Elaborate.

_____

_____

_____

_____

_____

_____

Action Plan

1. Adopt Ellyn Satter's "Division of Responsibility" around eating. According to Satter, it's a parent's job to decide what food is offered, where it is offered when it is offered. The child's job is whether and how much to eat of what's offered.

2. Minimizing anxiety around food should be more important than food consumption.

3. Know that it is essential to pay attention to your kid's feelings while they are eating.

Self-Evaluation

What new did you learn in this chapter? Did the action plan help in easing the food time struggles?

_____

_____

_____

_____

_____

_____

_____

_____

_____

_____

_____

_____

_____

_____

_____

_____

_____

_____

_____

Chapter 23:
Consent

Chapter Overview

The chapter discusses how bodily consent is just as much an issue for children as it is for adults. Your kids need to learn to set boundaries and communicate them effectively to others. They must not keep sacrificing their needs for the sake of others.

Read ahead to understand more about consent.

Goal Statement

"I will help my kids set firm boundaries around their bodies by teaching them to say No."

Chapter Summary

You are in charge of your body and who touches it, when, and for how long. The same goes for your children. They should be confidently able to set boundaries around their bodies and communicate that effectively to others. We are often taught to set aside our own feelings for the sake of making others happy. You shouldn't do that with your kid. Instead, when your kid behaves in a certain manner, you must demonstrate empathy by believing in your kid's experience. Otherwise, they will develop self-doubt.

Here are a few strategies to establish consent as a baseline rule for your kids –

1. **I believe you** - When you say that you trust them, the kids learn to trust themselves as well. This empowers them to take their own decisions and set boundaries.

2. **You're the only one in your body** - This is another way to demonstrate trust in your child. You can use the phrases like- "You're the only one in your body, so you know best what's going inside you."

3. **Socratic Questioning** - You can try asking thought-provoking questions related to consent to your kids. You can refer to the original book for a few ideas but you must come up with your own questions to make the experience more useful.

Check for Understanding

1. Kids can never be in charge of their bodies.

    TRUE   **FALSE**

2. You cannot trust what your child feels is going inside them.

    TRUE   **FALSE**

3. Showing empathy for your kids' experiences develops self-doubt in them.

    TRUE   **FALSE**

4. You must not always set aside your feelings just for the sake of others.

    TRUE   **FALSE**

Reflection Questions

1. How important is consent in your family system? Justify with examples.

_____

_____

_____

_____

_____

_____

_____

2. Do you think that your kids should keep sacrificing their own needs to make others happy? Why, or why not?

_____

_____

_____

_____

_____

_____

_____

3. How do you react when your kid's and your needs clash? Cite some examples.

_____

_____

_____

_____

_____

_____

_____

4. Do you agree with the idea that your kid is in charge of their body? Why, or why not?

_____

_____

_____

_____

_____

_____

_____

Action Plan

1. Say to yourself – It's not my job to make other people happy. I don't have to give up on my needs to take care of them.
2. Never encourage your kids to always set aside their feelings in favor of making other people happy.
3. Respond empathetically to your child in tough situations. It will build the circuitry for consent instead of self-doubt.

Self-Evaluation

What did you learn about consent in this chapter? Did the action plan prove helpful?

_____

_____

_____

_____

_____

_____

_____

_____

_____

_____

_____

_____

_____

_____

_____

_____

_____

_____

_____

_____

_____

_____

_____

_____

Chapter 24:
Tears

Chapter Overview

The chapter discusses the significance of tears in expressing one's emotional state. While your kid's tears might trigger you into a reactive state, you need to be more empathetic and considerate towards your kid.

Read ahead to understand more about the significance of tears.

Goal Statement

"I will learn to react better to my kid's tears by being more empathetic towards them."

Chapter Summary

While tears are universal, our reactions to them aren't. They are based on how our experiences shape our circuitry. If you are tearing up, it's a sign that you need emotional support and connection from others. Also, a kid's tears are a manifestation of a child's vulnerability. It can be triggering for you if you were taught to shut down your support needs. You react to them in the way you were reacted to.

Additionally, when your child shows distress, you might assume it to be your fault and failure, triggering guilt inside you. It is not. And whatever you feel, you must always respect your kid's tears. This would come from believing in the inherent goodness of your kids. As an adult, you must overreact at times when people are showing disinterest, invalidation, or minimization of your feelings. The same goes for the kids. Remember that showing empathy doesn't mean you have to give in to all your kid's demands.

Here are a few strategies for you to use –

1. **Talk about tears** - Talk about tears to your kids when they are not crying. This will de-shame the crying experience.

2. **Connect tears with the importance** - Tell your kids that tears are a sign that something important is going on and they need to pay attention to it.

3. **Socratic Questioning** - Encouraging kids to think deeply about tears and challenge the common narratives about tears and showing vulnerability.

Check for Understanding

1. Tears are how your kids manipulate you.

   TRUE　　　　　**FALSE**

2. Kids should never be allowed to show vulnerability.

   TRUE　　　　　**FALSE**

3. The way your parents reacted to your tears has an impact on how you react to your kids'.

   TRUE　　　　　**FALSE**

4. Showing empathy doesn't mean you have to give in to your kid's demands.

   TRUE　　　　　**FALSE**

Reflection Questions

1. How do you feel about your tears? Elaborate.

_____

_____

_____

_____

_____

_____

_____

2. When do you over-escalate your emotions? Cite real-life experiences.

_____

_____

_____

_____

_____

_____

_____

3. What is your reaction when your kid cries? What thoughts and feelings rise inside you at that moment?

_____

_____

_____

_____

_____

_____

_____

4. What was your childhood household like? Did your parents embrace vulnerability or reject it?

_____

_____

_____

_____

_____

_____

Action Plan

1. Tell yourself – I don't have to like my or my kid's tears, but I have to respect them.
2. Actively de-shame the crying experience for your kid.
3. Be curious about your kid's tears instead of being judgmental.

Self-Evaluation

What new did you learn about tears in this chapter? Did the action plan help you understand their tears better?

_____

_____

_____

_____

_____

Chapter 25:
Building Confidence

Chapter Overview

The chapter talks about confidence in detail, separating what it is from what it is not. Then it goes on to discuss various strategies that you can employ to build up confidence in your kid.

Read ahead to understand self-confidence in detail.

Goal Statement

"I will learn to build confidence in my kid by setting them up with self-trust."

Chapter Summary

People often define confidence as feeling good about oneself. But it doesn't mean that. Instead, it signifies our ability to feel at home with ourselves even in the widest range of feelings. So, when your kid is having a tough feeling, let them have their feeling instead of trying to convince them otherwise. It would teach them to trust their feelings inside them.

Another aspect of confidence is seeking internal validation instead of external validation. Even your well-intentioned phrases might motivate them to seek approval from others rather than themselves.

Here are a few strategies that you can employ to build confidence in your kids –

1. **Lead with validation -** The strategy involves showing your kids that you see their feelings as real and manageable. The child must understand that their feelings are okay.

2. **"How'd you Think to"? -** When you show your kids that you are curious about them, it builds up their capacity to self-reflect.

3. **Inside stuff over outside stuff -** When you focus on what's inside a child in terms of their enduring qualities, fears, and ideas, you build their circuitry for self-confidence.

4. **"It's okay how you feel" -** Self-confidence comes from self-trust. If your child can trust their own feelings to be okay, they can take a firm stand corresponding to those feelings.

Check for Understanding

1. Confidence is about feeling good about oneself.
   TRUE   **FALSE**

2. Your child needs to understand that it is not okay for them to show their feelings.
   TRUE   **FALSE**

3. When you focus on the inside stuff, you set your children up for self-confidence.
   TRUE   **FALSE**

4. Confident people seek internal validation instead of external validation.
   TRUE   **FALSE**

Reflection Questions

1. What are the qualities of a confident person according to you?

_____

_____

_____

_____

_____

_____

_____

2. Do you think your child is self-confident? Why, or why not?

_____

_____

_____

_____

_____

_____

3. With your kids, do you focus more on what's inside them or what they show outside (their behavior, achievements, etc.)? Justify with examples.

_____

_____

_____

_____

_____

_____

_____

4. When your kids express a hard feeling, do you acknowledge it or try to shove it away? Cite real-life examples.

_____

_____

_____

_____

_____

_____

_____

Action Plan

1. Allow your kid to have a feeling and own it. Actively seek to teach it to them.
2. You have to say the right things to your kid both when things go wrong, and when things go right.
3. Teach your kids to be more curious about themselves and explore more with self-reflection.
4. Teach them to focus more on their efforts than their accomplishments. Show them that their efforts are necessary.

Self-Evaluation

What new did you learn about confidence in this chapter? Did the action plan enable you to help your kid with their confidence?

_____

_____

_____

_____

_____

_____

_____

_____

_____

_____

_____

_____

_____

_____

_____

_____

_____

_____

_____

_____

_____

_____

_____

Chapter 26:
Perfectionism

Chapter Overview

The chapter talks about how perfectionist tendencies might be making your kids give up as soon as they start struggling with a task. For them, behavior is an indicator of identity, and they aren't comfortable being good enough. Thus, instead of trying harder, they just give up the task in the middle.

Read ahead to understand perfectionism in your kids in detail.

Goal Statement

"I will help my kids persevere by relating better to their perfectionism."

Chapter Summary

Some kids cannot tolerate good enough. They shut down if things go even slightly different from how they imagined. The difference between the imagined and the real manifests as perfectionism. It's a struggle for emotional regulation.

Perfectionist kids also are prone to rigidity and extreme moods. They are either on top of the world, or bottom of the barrel. There's no in-between. Their self-concept is very fragile as there's a very narrow lane when they feel good about themselves. Your goal as a parent is to widen this lane.

For perfectionists, behavior is an indicator of identity. You have to teach them to separate what they do from who they are. They need to find their worth outside success. That's why you should help your kid to get better at relating to their perfectionism. Remember that it doesn't have to be eradicated completely as some traits like drive, strong-mindedness and conviction are going to take your kids a long way.

Here are a few strategies to manage your kid's perfectionism –

1. **Make your own mistakes** - Be mindful of making errors and struggling around your kids. Model it for them that it is okay to make mistakes and not be perfect.
2. **See the feeling underneath perfectionism** - See and speak the feeling underneath your kid's perfectionism aloud. It will help them build self-awareness.
3. **Stuffed Animal Play** - Use stuffed animal plays to teach your kids that it is okay to not be perfect.
4. **Introduce the Perfect Voice** - Introduce the idea that people often have a perfect girl/boy inside them who wants everything to be perfect. But you shouldn't let that voice overpower you. Acknowledge it but never let it dictate.
5. **Do a 180 on Perfectionism** - Device games that reward not-knowing and learning, rather than knowing it all and doing things perfectly.

Check for Understanding

1. You should strive to relate to your perfectionism instead of completely rejecting it.

   TRUE   **FALSE**

2. Perfectionist kids have milder moods.

   TRUE   **FALSE**

3. Perfectionists tend to shut down when things don't go their way even in the slightest.

   TRUE   **FALSE**

4. For perfectionists, behavior is an indicator of identity.

   TRUE   **FALSE**

5. Kids must not find their worth outside success.

   TRUE   **FALSE**

Reflection Questions

1. Can your kid tolerate good enough or are they a perfectionist? Justify with examples.

   _____

   _____

   _____

   _____

   _____

   _____

   _____

2. What are your views on perfectionism?

   _____

   _____

   _____

   _____

   _____

_____

_____

3. *One's behavior is not an indicator of one's identity* – Do you agree?
   Why, or why not?

_____

_____

_____

_____

_____

_____

4. Do you encourage your kids to make their own mistakes or simply
   solve their issues for them? Do you act judgmental and reactive when
   they make a mistake? Justify with examples.

_____

_____

_____

_____

_____

_____

_____

Action plan

1. Adopt a mantra that encourages your kid when they make a mistake. The mantra shouldn't be something pushing you to improve but something that is along the line of – 'It is okay to make mistakes. I am good and worthy even when I make mistakes."
2. Make a game of not-knowing. Make it a goal to make mistakes and give high fives for errors.

Self-Evaluation

What new did you learn about perfectionism in this chapter? Did the action plan enable you to help your kid relate better to their perfectionist tendencies?

_____

_____

_____

_____

_____

_____

_____

_____

_____

_____

_____

_____

Chapter 27:
Separation Anxiety

Chapter Overview

The chapter talks about the separation anxiety that kids often have while separating from their parents during school time, trips, and other such occasions. It is normal for kids to be upset about being separated from their parents. Parents' presence signifies safety that kids want to cling to.

Read ahead to understand more about your kid's separation anxiety.

Goal Statement

"I will help my kid develop a mental representation of our relationship so that they can feel safe even in my absence."

Chapter Summary

Separation is tough and there's nothing wrong with a child who struggles with it. If your child clings to you in a moment of separation, it is because the behavior is rooted in attachment. For a calmer separation moment, they first need to trust that they are safe in the world even when their parents are not next to them. This can happen when children create a mental representation of the parent-child relationship so that they can access it wherever they are.

Remember that it is key that you do not label one kind of separation behavior as better than the other. Each child is going to have their own experiences.

Here are a few strategies for you to manage your kid's separation anxiety —

1. **Check in with your own anxiety** - If you yourself are anxious while separating from your kid, it's a given that they will absorb your energy and feel anxious.
2. **Talk about separation in advance** - Talk to your kid about separation before it happens.
3. **Routine + Practice** - Practice saying goodbyes regularly with your kid. Such dry runs will make it an easier experience for you and your kid when the actual thing happens.
4. **Transitional object** - Transitional objects like stuffed animals, family pictures, etc., can help your kid feel your presence even when you are not there.
5. **Telling the story** - Once the separation is over, talk to your kid about how the moment of separation felt. Talk about their experience afterward. It would remind them that the moment of separation doesn't color their entire experience.

Check for Understanding

1. It's abnormal for kids to cry when separating from their parents for the first time.

    TRUE   **FALSE**

2. Parents should keep their own anxieties in check when separating from their kids.

   TRUE   **FALSE**

3. Talking to kids about separation can serve to prepare them in advance.

   TRUE   **FALSE**

4. When kids start to believe that they are in a safe world, they show less separation anxiety.

   TRUE   **FALSE**

Reflection Questions

1. How do your kids behave when you drop them off at school? Cite real-life experiences.

   _____

   _____

   _____

   _____

   _____

   _____

   _____

2. What goes inside you when you get separated from your kid? How do you react?

   _____

   _____

   _____

   _____

_____

_____

_____

3. What is your view on separation anxiety?

_____

_____

_____

_____

_____

_____

Action Plan

1. Give your kid a transitional object like a stuffed toy, a blanket, or something that can remind them of your presence even when you are absent.

2. Practice saying goodbyes to your kid.

3. Don't label your kid's separation behavior as good or bad. It is just what it is.

4. Employ all the strategies listed in the chapter for better results.

Self-Evaluation

What new did you learn about your kid's separation anxiety in this chapter? Did the action plan prove helpful?

_____

_____

_____

_____

_____

_____

_____

_____

_____

_____

_____

_____

_____

_____

_____

_____

_____

_____

_____

_____

_____

_____

_____

_____

_____

Chapter 28:
Sleep

Chapter Overview

The chapter discusses your kid's sleep patterns in detail along with what might be disrupting them. If your kid struggles with sleeping at bedtime, this chapter underlines the causes and the strategies that you can use to help them.

Read ahead to understand how your kids can sleep better.

Goal Statement

"I will help my kids sleep better by ensuring that they feel safe even in my absence."

Chapter Summary

Kids' sleep struggles are challenging for parents to handle as they are desperate for rest at the end of the day. This might make them reactive in the face of the challenge. You must understand though that sleep struggles are ultimately separation struggles. Your child must feel safe enough to separate from you and let their body drift to sleep.

Sleep is also a time when kids might express accumulated anxieties from other aspects of their lives. If not resolved, these stressors might lead to sleep disruptions. To help your kid, you first have to help them build their coping skills during the day when the stakes are lower.

Once they can do that, you can attempt strategies for a smoother bedtime experience.

If your child struggles while separating, it just means that they are unable to internalize the soothing aspects of a parent-child relationship.

Here is a list of a few strategies that you can use –

1. **Where is Everyone? -** Talk to your kid about your routine when they are asleep. Let them know that you're still there even when they are asleep.

2. **Examine your daytime separation routine -** Try to build the separation skills in your kid during the day when their bodies are much more receptive to learning.

3. **Role-play -** Use stuffed toys to role-play your kid's bedtime routine. Add elements to infuse a sense of parental availability even when the kids are asleep.

4. **Infuse your presence -** You have to infuse your presence into your child's room so that they can feel it even when you are not there.

5. **Mantras for you and your child -** Give your child mantras that they can repeat again and again to infuse your presence, comfort, and confidence. The mantra can be in a "singsongy" voice to make it more soothing.

6. **The safe distance method -** Gradually increase the distance between you and your kid over nights until you are eventually out of their room. This will prepare them to separate from you in a smoother manner.

7. **The comfort button -** You can get a recordable button with at least thirty seconds of recording space. You can record a soothing message

in your voice that will make your child feel your presence. Make it a rule for your kid to use it at least a few times, before calling you when they feel alone.

Check for Understanding

1. Sleep struggles are a symptom of an underlying need or unresolved issues.

   TRUE   **FALSE**

2. You can help your kid sleep better by infusing your presence into their surroundings.

   TRUE   **FALSE**

3. Your child's separation coping skills have an impact on their sleeping patterns.

   TRUE   **FALSE**

Reflection Questions

1. What's your kid's sleeping pattern like? Cite real-life examples.

_____

_____

_____

_____

_____

_____

_____

2. Does your child struggle when separating from you? Elaborate with examples.

_____

_____

_____

_____

_____

_____

3. Does your child express feelings of being anxious about other aspects of life? How do you react or help them out?

_____

_____

_____

_____

_____

_____

Action Plan

1. Ensure that you care for yourself as well. Otherwise, you might become reactive and that will in turn make the sleep struggles of your kid even more intensified.

2. Put some pictures of you and family photos in your kid's room. You can do the same with your room if you feel anxious while separating from your kid.

3. After they fall asleep, write down a note or make a drawing with their name on it and put it next to their bed while they are asleep. When they wake up at midnight, they will know that you are still there even when they sleep.

Self-Evaluation

What did you learn about your kid's sleeping challenges in this chapter? Did the action plan enable you to help your child?

_____

_____

_____

_____

_____

_____

_____

_____

_____

_____

_____

_____

_____

_____

_____

_____

Chapter 29:
Kids who don't like talking about feelings (Deeply Feeling Kids)

Chapter Overview

The chapter talks about the kids who feel and react more intensely than their peers of the same age. They have deep fears about their lovability and thus do not like to show vulnerability in any situation. Vulnerability makes them feel ashamed, something humans totally want to avoid.

Read ahead to understand more about the deeply feeling kids and how you can help them.

Goal Statement

"I will learn to help my Deeply feeling kid to open up more by de-shaming vulnerability for them."

Chapter Summary

Some kids feel more deeply than others. That's why they get activated more quickly than others. It doesn't mean that there's anything wrong with them or you. With such DFKs (Deep Feeling Kids), you often need a different set of strategies as they often struggle to accept help. The first step to approaching these kids in highly emotional situations is to set aside any blame and bring out your compassion both towards them and yourself.

These kids often shut down their feelings as vulnerability sits right next to shame for them. Thus they simply start pushing others away by whatever means necessary. They have deep fears about their badness and unlovability. And when their reactions evoke rejection and invalidation from their parents, their worst fears come true. It means that the parents also get overwhelmed by the situation and their worst fears come true. That's why you must focus on their struggle rather than their behavior.

Here are a few strategies that can enable you to help your deep-feeling kids –

1. **Move from blame to curiosity** - Be curious about your kid's feelings rather than blaming yourself or them.

2. **Containment First** - Know that your primary goal is to keep the child safe by ensuring containment. In tough situations, they need you to be a sturdy leader.

3. **"You're a good kid having a hard time"** - DFks pick up your perception of them even more in the difficult moments. So, you need to hold a good version of them in your mind and act empathetically. If they sense rejection, their fears will be proven true. Instead, imagine them as a kid who is in pain and fear.

4. **Be present and wait it out** - If you can think of nothing, at least, just be there. Your loving and calming presence is all your kid needs to calm down. It shows them that you're not overwhelmed by them and that they are good and lovable.

5. **Thumbs Up/ Down/ to the Side -** If your kid doesn't like to talk about feelings, you can ask them to use thumb signals to communicate their emotions in a tough emotional situation.

Check for Understanding

1. DFKs are bad kids who love troubling their parents.

   TRUE   **FALSE**

2. Deep-feeling kids often shut their own feelings down.

   TRUE   **FALSE**

3. Shaming your kids regularly can make them resistant to shame.

   TRUE   **FALSE**

4. You should hold a positive perception of your kid.

   TRUE   **FALSE**

5. DFks are doomed to have sad life as adults.

   TRUE   **FALSE**

Reflection Questions

1. Do you have a kid that matches the criteria of a DFK? Justify with real-life experiences.

_____

_____

_____

_____

_____

_____

_____

2. How do you manage when your kid throws extended and violent tantrums?

_____

_____

_____

_____

_____

_____

3. Do you start blaming yourself or the kid in their tough emotional moment? How does it play out?

_____

_____

_____

_____

_____

_____

4. How open are your kids to you about their emotional matters? Justify with real-life examples.

_____

_____

_____

_____

_____

_____

5. Does your household welcome emotional expression by family
   members? Or does everyone keep their emotional matters to
   themselves? Elaborate.

_____

_____

_____

_____

_____

_____

Action Plan

1. Whenever in a highly emotionally charged situation with your DFK,
   notice the mode you are in. You must avoid the blame mode and
   enter the curiosity mode.

2. Remind yourself to contain the situation first, and correct it later.
   Remember that your primary job is to keep your kid safe.

3. In tough situations, repeat to yourself, "He/She is a good kid having
   a hard time." Repeat it as many times as you need to believe it. Tell
   it to your kid if you want to.

Self-Evaluation

What did you learn about Deep feeling kids in this chapter? Did the action plan help?

_____

_____

_____

_____

_____

_____

_____

_____

_____

_____

_____

_____

_____

_____

_____

_____

_____

_____

_____

_____

_____

_____

_____

_____

_____

Reference A

Check for Understanding Answer Key

Chapter 1 Answer Key

1. FALSE   2. FALSE   3. TRUE   4. TRUE   5. FALSE

Chapter 2 Answer Key

1. FALSE   2. FALSE   3. TRUE   4. TRUE   5. TRUE

Chapter 3 Answer Key

1. FALSE   2. TRUE   3. FALSE   4. TRUE

Chapter 4 Answer Key

1. FALSE   2. TRUE   3. TRUE   4. TRUE   5. TRUE

Chapter 5 Answer Key

1. FALSE   2. TRUE   3. TRUE   4. TRUE

Chapter 6 Answer Key

1. FALSE   2. FALSE   3. TRUE   4. TRUE

Chapter 7 Answer Key

1. FALSE   2. TRUE   3. TRUE   4. FALSE

Chapter 8 Answer Key

1. TRUE   2. TRUE   3. TRUE   4. TRUE

Chapter 9 Answer Key

1. FALSE   2. FALSE   3. FALSE   4. FALSE

Chapter 10 Answer Key

1. FALSE   2. FALSE   3. TRUE   4. TRUE

Chapter 11 Answer Key

1. TRUE   2. TRUE   3. FALSE   4. FALSE

Chapter 12 Answer Key

1. FALSE   2. FALSE   3. TRUE   4. FALSE

Chapter 13 Answer Key

1. FALSE   2. TRUE   3. FALSE   4. TRUE

Chapter 14 Answer Key

1. FALSE   2. FALSE   3. FALSE   4. FALSE

Chapter 15 Answer Key

1. TRUE   2. TRUE   3. TRUE   4. TRUE

Chapter 16 Answer Key

1. TRUE   2. FALSE   3. FALSE   4. TRUE

Chapter 17 Answer Key

1. FALSE   2. TRUE   3. TRUE   4. FALSE

Chapter 18 Answer Key

1. TRUE   2. TRUE   3. FALSE   4. FALSE   5. FALSE

Chapter 19 Answer Key

1. FALSE   2. FALSE   3. FALSE   4. FALSE

Chapter 20 Answer Key

1. FALSE   2. TRUE   3. TRUE   4. FALSE

Chapter 21 Answer Key

1. FALSE   2. FALSE   3. TRUE

Chapter 22 Answer Key

1. FALSE   2. TRUE   3. TRUE   4. FALSE

Chapter 23 Answer Key

1. FALSE   2. FALSE   3. FALSE   4. TRUE

Chapter 24 Answer Key

1. FALSE   2. FALSE   3. TRUE   4. TRUE

Chapter 25 Answer Key

1. FALSE   2. FALSE   3. TRUE   4. TRUE

Chapter 26 Answer Key

1. TRUE   2. FALSE   3. TRUE   4. TRUE   5. FALSE

Chapter 27 Answer Key

1. FALSE   2. TRUE   3. TRUE   4. TRUE

Chapter 28 Answer Key

1. TRUE   2. TRUE   3. TRUE

Chapter 29 Answer Key

1. FALSE   2. TRUE   3. FALSE   4. TRUE   5. FALSE

About the author
Becky Kennedy

Dr. Becky Kennedy is a mom and clinical psychologist, popular for simplifying kids' issues for parents to understand. She also runs a weekly podcast – Good Inside Us with Dr. Becky – which is very popular among parents of kids of all ages. Her ultimate goal is to equip parents with the knowledge and the tools to raise kids in a more empathetic and healthy manner. She has done her Ph.D. in clinical psychology from Columbia University.

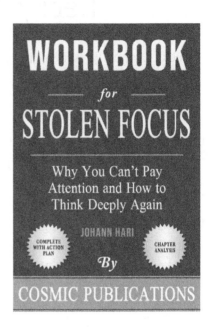

THANK YOU FOR FINISHING THE BOOK!

Looks like you've enjoyed it! :)

We here at Cosmic Publications will always strive to deliver to you the highest quality guides. So, we would like to thank you for supporting us and
reading until the very end.

Before you go, would you mind leaving us a review on Amazon? It will mean a lot to us and support us creating high quality guides for you in the future.
Just scan the QR code below.

Thank you again.

Warmly,

The Cosmic Publications Team

Scan me

COSMIC
PUBLICATIONS

Made in the USA
Las Vegas, NV
27 September 2024

95883790R00118